CEREAL PROCESSING

Food Cycle Technology Source Books

CEREAL PROCESSING

Practical Action Publishing Ltd
27a Albert Street, Rugby, CV21 2SG, Warwickshire, UK
www.practicalactionpublishing.org

This edition published 1994 \Digitised 2008

ISBN 978 1 85339 136 1

Since 1974, Practical Action Publishing has published and disseminated books and information in support of international development work throughout the world. Practical Action Publishing is a trading name of Practical Action Publishing Ltd (Company Reg. No. 1159018), the wholly owned publishing company of Practical Action. Practical Action Publishing trades only in support of its parent charity objectives and any profits are covenanted back to Practical Action (Charity Reg. No. 247257, Group VAT Registration No. 880 9924 76).

Illustrations by Peter Dobson
Typeset by Inforum, Rowlands Castle, Hants, UK

Preface

This source book is one of a continuing UNIFEM series which aims to increase awareness of the range of technological options and sources of expertise, as well as indicating the complex nature of designing and successfully implementing technology development and dissemination programmes.

UNIFEM was established in 1976, and is an autonomous body associated since 1984 with the United Nations Development Programme. UNIFEM seeks to free women from under-productive tasks and augment the productivity of their work as a means of accelerating the development process. It does this through funding specific women's projects which yield direct benefits and through actions directed to ensure that all development policies, plans, programmes and projects take account of the needs of women producers.

In recognition of women's special roles in the production, processing, storage, preparation and marketing of food, UNIFEM initiated a Food Cycle Technology project in 1985 with the aim of promoting the widespread diffusion of tested technologies to increase the productivity of women's labour in this sector. While global in perspective, the initial phase of the project was implemented in Africa in view of the concern over food security in many countries of the region.

A careful evaluation of the Africa experience in the final phase of this five-year programme showed that there was a need for catalytic interventions which would lead to an enabling environment for women to have easier access to technologies. This would be an environment where women producers can obtain information on the available technologies, have the capacity to analyse such information, make technological choices on their own, and acquire credit and training to enable the purchase and operation of the technology of their choice. This UNIFEM source book series aims to facilitate the building of such an environment.

Acknowledgements

This series of food cycle technology source books has been prepared at Intermediate Technology (IT) in the United Kingdom within the context of UNIFEM's Women and Food Cycle Technologies specialization.

During the preparation process the project staff contacted numerous project directors, rural development agencies, technology centres, women's organizations, equipment manufacturers and researchers in all parts of the world.

The authors wish to thank the many agencies and individuals who have contributed to the preparation of this source book. Special thanks are owed to the International Labour Organization (ILO), the Food and Agriculture Organization of the United Nations (FAO), the United Nations Children's Fund (UNICEF), the Economic Commission for Africa (ECA), the German Appropriate Technology Exchange (GATE/GTZ), the *Groupe de Recherche et d'Echanges Technologiques* (GRET), the Royal Tropical Institute (KIT), the International Development Research Centre (IDRC), the Natural Resources Institute (NRI), Appropriate Technology International (ATI), the Institute of Development Studies at Sussex University (IDS), and the Save the Children Fund.

The preparation of the source books was funded by UNIFEM with a cost-sharing contribution from the Government of Italy and the Government of the Netherlands. UNIFEM is also grateful to the Government of Italy, via the Italian Association of Women in Development (AIDOS), for sponsoring the translation of this series into French and Portuguese, and the printing of the first editions.

Barrie Axtell
IT Consultants

Els Kocken
UNIFEM

Ruby Sandhu
UNIFEM

Contents

Introduction

CEREAL GRAINS are the seeds of cultivated grasses and all have a rather similar structure. This forms, with minor variations, the basis for their processing.

Towards the base of the grain is the germ or embryo from which a new plant can develop, surrounded by the endosperm which is a starchy body providing nourishment for the developing embryo. The whole grain is surrounded by protective covering layers which include the testa and pericarp. A number of different words are used to describe the various parts of a grain, which can be somewhat confusing. The essential point to remember is that a grain has four main components: the germ, the starchy interior, nutritious outer layers and the external fibrous husk.

This source book concentrates on four cereal grains of great importance in many developing countries: maize (corn), paddy (rice), sorghum, and millet. While wheat is also a very important cereal, in Africa (for which this source book was originally intended) it tends to be grown in large farms and processed into flour in large-scale mills. As such it falls outside the scope of the book.

While each type of cereal requires a specific post-harvest treatment, there are certain general principles that may be applied to all. Cereals pass through a number of stages in a long and sometimes complex chain from harvest to consumption. This is often referred to as the total post-harvest system, and is shown in the flow diagram. It is most important to understand that the total system falls into three distinct areas. The first covers harvesting up to the storage of the grain. The second — primary processing — involves the further treatment of the grain, but the products are still not directly consumable. Before consumption, grains from primary processing need to pass through a secondary processing stage such as baking.

Projects may therefore involve only one or several of the activities in the total chain, such as the growing of corn and its subsequent treatment right through to selling corn tortillas, or simply the purchase of wheat flour and the baking of bread.

This source book looks at all these stages, although secondary processing steps such as baking are not covered in detail.

TOTAL POST-HARVEST CEREAL SYSTEM

HARVESTING
↓
PRE-DRYING IN FIELD
↓
THRESHING
↓
WINNOWING
↓
DRYING
↓
STORAGE OF GRAIN
↓
PRIMARY PROCESSING
cleaning, grading, hulling, pounding, milling, grinding, tempering, soaking, parboiling, drying, sieving
↓
SECONDARY PROCESSING
baking, frying, extruding, blending, fermenting, roasting
↓
PACKAGING, MARKETING
↓
UTILIZATION BY CUSTOMER

Much of the food grain harvested in the tropics is lost through inadequate handling, storage and processing techniques. A wealth of data on these losses has been published which is often conflicting or site-specific. The Food and Agricultural Organization of the UN (FAO) estimates global losses of 10 per cent and the Danish NGO, DANIDA, found that 22 per cent of field losses of maize in Nigeria were caused by insect and fungal attack. Early harvesting of rice to catch the market can result in a 10 per cent loss of yield (FAO, undated). As well as physical loss, there is loss in quality and factors affecting nutritional value and conservation to be considered. The common points at which post-harvest losses occur are listed below:

o vermin and insect infestation during the whole of the post-harvest chain;
o yield losses due to early harvesting;
o grain losses due to transport of un-threshed material;
o physical losses at threshing;
o incorrect moisture levels for threshing, milling and grinding;
o physical losses due to poor primary and secondary processing techniques.

After looking at these stages in the total system, this source book examines improvements that can be made to reduce some of the time, labour, and losses associated with the post-harvest processing of cereals. One important point must be borne in mind when looking to reduce post-harvest grain losses. Care must be taken to ensure that the losses are real. In some cases it has been found that losses to the mill-owner are gains to the poorest, who pick up the split grains. The same can be true for transporting from the field. An 'improved' system, therefore, may lead to greater impoverishment. The economics of an improvement can look more or less attractive depending on how

far the net is cast. Traditional post-harvest systems are often very efficient when placed within the context of the complete socio-economic system. Marginal improvements to post-harvest activities are often more effective than radical changes.

There are other important considerations when introducing changes to post-harvest systems. If improvements are going to cost money, can women afford the improvements or will they need credit? Will the improvements earn enough to repay the credit? Many changes have in the past led to women losing control over part of the productive process and thus have increased their poverty. If changes mean that women have to organize on a co-operative or group basis, do they have the necessary skills, experience, and social structure or will they require training in organization management, and quality and financial control?

When new products are being introduced, careful consideration has to be given to the marketing aspects: where are the markets, how big are they, how will goods be transported to market, how should the goods be packaged, what is the competition? (See Chapter 5 for more detail on these questions.)

Some areas of the post-harvest system such as drying and storage are discussed with specific reference to cereals; however, there are books covering drying and storage in greater detail which should be read in conjunction with this source book.

Before the processing of cereals is discussed, a note on their nutritional value is important. Because cereal grains are available and affordable, they are, for the majority of the people in developing countries, a major proportion of their diet. Carbohydrates and protein are the two main constituents by weight in any grain and they offer, after water, the two most important substances for our survival:

energy and protein. Protein can be more readily obtained from fish, meat and dairy produce, however, and, apart from having a greater proportion of protein by weight than cereal grains, they also have an excellent balance of the essential amino acids the body needs for survival.

Cereal grains lack, in particular, one essential amino acid, lysine. When expensive protein sources are unobtainable, beans (which are rich in lysine) are often used to supplement cereal grains.

As children require a higher proportion by weight of protein than adults, the protein:energy ratio becomes very significant. Young children cannot eat enough of a cereal dish to obtain their quota of protein, because of the bulkiness of processed cereals. Supplementing the diet with a good quality protein source is therefore essential, especially to ensure sufficient intake of lysine.

However, the lack of high-protein foods and their high prices are limiting factors for people existing on diets near subsistence level. The significance of cereal grain protein and carbohydrate for these people cannot be overstressed.

Consideration must be given to the effect of processing on the chemical composition of cereal products and hence their nutritional value. The various nutrients are distributed unevenly throughout the different parts of the grain (germ, endosperm, seed coat and fruit coat layers etc.), and there is also a different pattern of distribution between different types of cereal grains. There is,

therefore, no hard and fast rule regarding loss of nutrients upon processing. It should be borne in mind that the most important effects of processing on nutritional value are brought about by the following:

○ the separation and removal of parts of the grain, leaving only a fraction of the whole grain as the product, constitutes a loss in nutrients;
○ parts of the grain being discarded (as above) may bring about a concentration of certain nutrients (i.e. increasing their proportion by weight of the product);
○ processing treatments may themselves bring about changes in nutrients (e.g. germination, fermentation, parboiling);
○ the removal of the outer layers of the grain, while causing a loss in some nutrients, may be desirable. For example, tannin is concentrated in the outer layers of sorghum and its removal is nutritionally essential, and the milling of brown rice to white rice produces a product which is far easier to prepare.

Clearly, a publication of this size can only provide a general introduction to the large subject of cereals. Its purpose is to give readers a broad understanding, and so reference to more detailed documents and consulting with technical specialists would be essential before becoming involved in any project implementation. A suggested reading list and sources of technical expertise are to be found at the back of the book.

1
Traditional post-harvest system

THIS SECTION DESCRIBES the steps involved in the traditional processing of cereals. It is vital that project planners and managers consider the traditional technologies in their particular socio-economic context before introducing any technical improvements or adaptations. The following main components of the post-harvest food system are discussed: harvesting, threshing and winnowing, drying, storage and primary processing methods.

Post-harvest grain losses are a major concern in the traditional system. This chapter deals with the traditional post-harvest system and local methods by which these losses are reduced. Chapter 2 describes some improved technologies which have been developed to further reduce losses and increase productivity in cereal processing, together with relevant technical background information. Most of the cereals discussed are processed in much the same way but, where relevant, differences between processing techniques are mentioned.

Harvesting

There is an optimum time for harvesting which depends upon the maturity of the crop and climatic conditions (FAO, 1970) and has a significant effect on the subsequent quality of the grain during storage. Harvesting often begins before the grain is fully ripe and extends until mould and insect damage are prevalent. Grain not fully ripened contains a higher proportion of moisture, and will deteriorate more quickly than mature grains because the enzyme systems are still active. If the grain remains in the field after maturity, repeated wetting from rain and dew at night, along with drying by the sun during the day, may cause grain to crack (particularly long-grain paddy) and increases the likelihood of insect damage (especially maize and paddy). Advice may therefore be necessary on the correct harvesting time.

Cereal crops are traditionally harvested manually, making high labour demands and therefore providing an important source of income for landless labourers.

Threshing and winnowing

Threshing is the removal of the grains from the rest of the plant. In the case of maize, the removal of the grain from the cob is referred to as shelling. Maize is shelled mainly with bare hands, by rubbing one cob against another. Most manual threshing methods use some implement; the simplest is a stick or hinged flail with which the crop, spread on the floor, is beaten. Such tools are simple and cheap but they are also laborious to use.

Threshing and shelling will contribute to losses if carried out in a manner that results in the cracking of grains. Other traditional methods of threshing, such as using animals to trample the sheaves on the threshing floor, or the modern equivalent using tractor wheels, may result in loss of unseparated grain. This method also allows impurities to become mixed with the grain, which may cause subsequent storage problems.

Winnowing involves separating the chaff from the grain. If there is plenty of wind, the threshed material is tossed in the air using forks, shovels or baskets. The lighter chaff and straw blow away while the heavy grains fall more or less vertically. Final cleaning may be done with a winnowing basket, which is shaken until any chaff and dust separate at the upper edge. An alternative method is to use winnowing sieves or open-weave baskets. Separating impurities from threshed grain can require almost as much labour as the original threshing.

Once threshed the grains must be dried and stored. In many cases, these two functions are performed together so that grain is dried during storage.

Drying

Drying the grain helps to prevent germination of seeds and the growth of bacteria and fungi, and considerably retards the development of mites and insects. With traditional methods, the rate and uniformity of drying is difficult to control, as it is dependent on environmental conditions. It is essential that food grains be dried quickly and effectively, but in most cases, regardless of the disadvantages, the small farmer still prefers sun-drying because it is cheap and simple.

Air is used as the drying medium, causing water to vaporize and conveying the moisture away from the grain. The moisture-carrying capacity of air is dependent upon its temperature, increasing with a rise in temperature (e.g. at 30°C the air is capable of holding twice as much moisture as at 16°C).

The simplest and most common method of drying is to lay the cut stalks on the ground in the fields, either in swathes of loose bundles or in stacks or heaps, until the crop is dry. When the plants are piled in large stacks they may suffer from a lack of circulating air, leading to sprouting, discoloration, and microbial damage. Sometimes racks are used for hanging unthreshed sorghum, millet, and paddy. Most racks are designed to permit air movement through the drying material.

At the homestead the crop is further dried by spreading on woven mats, hard surfaces (including roads), plastic sheets, or on the roof or ground. The drying time depends on the climatic conditions. Some farmers periodically turn or rake the grain during the drying period in order to obtain uniform drying. If it rains the crop must be protected. In other cases farmers dry their produce on raised platforms of various shapes. In Zambia, Malawi, and southern Tanzania, the platforms are shaped like a cone; in many other parts of Africa they are rectangular.

After drying many farmers store their produce in the home, where the smoke and heat produced during cooking helps complete the drying of the grain and reduces insect infestation. The smoke produced and heat lost in traditional cooking stoves thus serve a useful purpose which should not be ignored in the development of improved cooking stoves.

Storage

Traditional storage systems have evolved slowly within the limits of the local culture. Large amounts of grain for human consumption are stored in containers constructed of plant material, mud, or stones, often raised off the ground on platforms and protected from the weather by roofing material. The design and materials vary according to local resources and custom. In the humid areas of the Ivory Coast, Tanzania, and Kenya, maize is dried and stored

Table 1. Causes of losses in cereal processing

	Harvesting	*Threshing/shelling*	*Drying and storage*
Maize	Insects, birds, rodents	Incomplete stripping of cob Damage to grain	Inability to dry to correct moisture level leads to: Insects, rodents, birds Mould damage
Paddy	Delay leads to shattering Birds, rodents, insects	Breaking of grains Percentage of grain not shed Impurities become mixed with grain	Mould Discoloration Insects, rodents, birds Fermentation
Sorghum/ millet	Insects, birds, rodents	Breaking of grains Impurities become mixed with grain	Birds, insects, rodents

by suspending it in bundles from a tree, by hanging it on tacks, or by suspending it from poles. Because of the problems of rain and rodents and other predators, these methods are becoming less popular. In parts of East Africa and Central America, wood ash or rice husk ash is mixed with grain being stored to control infestation.

Storage conditions influence the rate of deterioration of grains. High temperatures and humidities encourage mould growth and provide conditions for rapid growth of insect populations. Deterioration is minimal in cool, dry areas, more marked in hot, dry ones, high in cool and damp conditions, and very high in hot, damp climates.

Table 1 lists specific loss factors before milling for maize, sorghum, millet, and paddy (NAS, 1978).

Primary processing methods

Whole grains store better than those ground into flour, so in many rural families women grind and pound only small amounts of grain for immediate consumption. Traditional grinding methods for various cereals are discussed below.

Maize

Maize may be either dry or wet milled. In dry milling, maize is usually ground between stones or by using a small hand-powered plate mill; otherwise custom or co-operatively owned power-driven hammer or plate mills are used. At other times, the grain is milled wet after it has been soaked and allowed to ferment slightly to improve its flavour. In Latin America maize is partially cooked in alkaline conditions to facilitate the removal of bran before it is milled. Where very small quantities are needed, the wet maize may be ground at home using a saddle stone or similar device. More commonly, hand- or power-driven plate mills are used to either roughly break the grain or mill it further to a smoother paste.

Maize grain can be pounded using a wooden pestle and mortar, or ground by hand using a quern (a rotating, hand-driven stone mill). The amount of maize required for several meals is taken off the cob and transferred to a wooden mortar. One or two cups of water are added and the whole is pounded.

If the maize meal is not used whole, it is transferred into a flat basket and shaken, so that the bran is separated from the floury endosperm. The flour is again collected into the mortar and pounded in the same way for three or four shorter periods, followed by the traditional separation of the bran. The resulting product is called 'pure' and the bran is often used to feed chickens.

Some of this 'pure' meal may be cooked as it is or with beans, but most undergoes further processing, such as soaking in water for one or two days until an odour develops owing to fermentation. Fermentation produces acidic conditions which inhibit the growth of undesirable bacteria. The water is then poured off, the soaked 'pure' meal is washed up to three times with fresh water, decanted, and again pounded in the mortar. It is then graded as before, into fine and coarse particles. The bigger particles are kept for further pounding until everything is reduced to a semolina-like flour. This product is ready for preparing into foods such as *uji* and *ugali*; it cannot be kept for more than a day. If dried it may be stored for a few weeks (Stewart, 1978). The shelf-life of maize meal is very short because maize has a relatively high fat content, which tends to go rancid quickly.

Paddy

In some countries paddy is parboiled before the husk is removed. Parboiling is partial cooking which causes the starch of the kernel to gelatinize, making it tougher. There is also a slight change in flavour which is preferred by some. The toughening process makes the seed more resistant to insect attack, to shattering during husking and to the absorption of moisture from the air. Paddy that has been parboiled has better nutritional quality owing to the migration of nutrients towards the centre of the grain during the process.

The parboiling process involves three stages:

o soaking or steeping of the paddy in cold or hot water to increase its moisture content;
o steaming to gelatinize the starch in the kernel;
o drying.

Traditional parboiling techniques differ greatly from country to country. In West Africa paddy is frequently parboiled in small quantities in earthenware pots or oil drums after soaking in cold water overnight. Sometimes the soaking water is brought to the boil, the fire extinguished, and the pot left overnight. The next day the water is drained off, a little fresh water added and the pot put over a fire until all the water evaporates. The paddy is then sun-dried. Traditional paddy parboiling techniques are slow and can only handle small quantities at a time.

The 'off' odours produced during prolonged steeping of the paddy in the first stage of parboiling has been recognized as a problem. Two methods of eliminating the offensive smell, which is caused mainly by microbial fermentation, are to reduce the steeping time by hot soaking (60–80°C) and to pre-steam the paddy before soaking, which reduces both the steeping time and the number of microorganisms in the paddy.

Careful drying after parboiling is essential to minimize post-harvest losses.

Husking paddy, which is sometimes referred to as de-husking or milling, is the process of removing the outer husk. Husked paddy is referred to as brown rice. Further milling of brown rice produces white rice. The most widespread traditional method uses a mortar and pestle. This may be carried out by one woman working by herself or by a number of women working in rhythm together. The method is very slow and laborious and output rarely exceeds 5kg per worker, per hour.

Hand-pounding produces an under-milled rice which is of greater nutritional value since it retains part of the bran which has high thiamine content and contains protein. Hand-pounding also results in a high proportion of broken kernels. Winnowing is carried out at intervals during this process (Mphuru, 1982).

Sorghum/millet

The outer layers of certain varieties of sorghum seed contain tannins which are slightly toxic, have a bitter taste and inhibit protein digestion when consumed. For these reasons sorghum is generally hulled (i.e. the outer layers are removed) and then pounded into flour.

Red or brown sorghum varieties continue to be grown in many parts of Africa, owing to their resistance to bird attack, in spite of the availability of white non-tannin varieties. Traditionally, the processing of sorghum and millet has been carried out by grinding the whole grain in querns, between stones, or by pounding the grain using a pestle and mortar. The last of these is the commonest method for sorghum. Once the seed has been winnowed to remove foreign matter, it is put in a large mortar and wetted. It is then pounded to strip the bran or 'shell' from the grain, followed by winnowing to remove the bran entirely. Pounding and winnowing are repeated several times before a good quality milled seed is obtained.

The milled seed is then washed with water to remove any small pieces of bran and soaked in water for 24 hours to 'condition' or 'temper' it. This is followed by drying to the correct moisture content and then re-grinding in a pestle and mortar. In order to obtain a good flour, sifting and pounding has to be repeated several times.

The flour obtained contains a large proportion of the oil-rich germ and the nutrients of the grain (Mphuru, 1982). Grains are moistened to facilitate the removal of the bran, but this can result in a slightly fermented flour. Although the keeping quality of this type of flour may be diminished because of fermentation, it has a modified flavour which is often considered desirable. The objective of hand-pounding is thus two-fold. In the first stage, the bran and pigmented layers are removed and in the second stage, the grain is pounded progressively, with intermittent sieving, into flour suitable for various end-products. These methods of hand-pounding are time-consuming and laborious and an output of only 1–3kg of flour per person per hour is possible.

2
Improved processes and technologies

In most developing countries, it is women who are largely responsible for the threshing, winnowing, drying, husking, shelling, and milling necessary to prepare grain for human consumption. These tasks are often arduous, monotonous, and time-consuming.

Care needs to be taken, however, regarding the introduction of new techniques into a rural community, in case they unintentionally worsen the women's situation instead of improving it. Although a technology may in theory lighten the women's workload it may lead to men taking over a task traditionally performed by women, so depriving them of income.

Harvesting

Crop harvesting equipment available to small-scale farmers in developing countries has changed little over the years. Knives, sickles and scythes continue to be the traditional tools used. Some low horsepower reapers are being developed, but because of their low capacity, high cost, and other problems, they are often not considered a suitable alternative to manual methods. The time at which a crop is harvested can have a significant effect on both the quantity of grain obtained and its quality.

Threshing

Although time-consuming and laborious, traditional manual and animal-powered threshing should not be dismissed out of hand. The problems of impurities and grain damage during manual threshing can be partially overcome with minor improvements; for example, carrying out the task in clean areas.

A range of small hand- and engine-driven mechanical threshers is available to improve not only the quality, in terms of damage and yield, but also the efficiency of human effort required. These fill the gap between traditional methods and highly sophisticated machines, which are mostly inappropriate for use by villagers owing to their high cost and maintenance problems.

Most mechanical threshers operate on the same basic principle, consisting of a cylinder or drum with teeth which strip the grain from the stalks as it passes between the revolving drum and a metal grate (known as the concave). Many of these machines have been developed for rice but can be used for other crops. However, it is reported that treadle operated machines are not suitable for threshing wheat as the power requirement is too great.

It is important to note that most mechanical threshers work best with grain dried to the correct moisture content. Under-drying leaves grain still attached to the stems; over-drying leads to excessive grain damage. Threshers are often classified according to the method of feeding, the design of the threshing drum/concave and the power source.

Feeding method

o **Hold-on:** the cut plants are held manually or mechanically in the threshing chamber until the grains have been detached by the rotating drum.
o **Throw-in:** the whole cut plants are fed into the machine.

Drum design

Peg tooth, rasp bar and wire loop threshers have small spikes or pegs, parallel bars or wire loops attached to the rotating cylinder as shown in the illustrations.

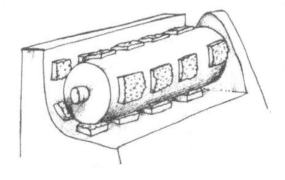

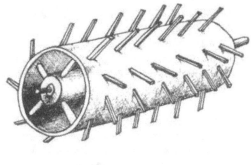

Rasp bar thresher

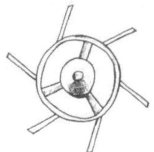

Peg tooth thresher

Power source

Human-powered mechanical threshers will typically have outputs of up to 200kg/hour (Mphuru, 1982). If outputs above this are required, the use of engine power is necessary.

Engine-powered models are obviously more expensive and have a greater capacity than manual and animal threshers. The majority of engine-powered threshers are throw-in, thus increasing the bulk which has to pass through the machine. There are two main types:

o **tangential flow** machines, in which the crop passes directly through the threshing chamber, around the circumference of the drum.

o **axial flow** machines, which have spirally positioned fins on the upper concave so that material fed in at one end

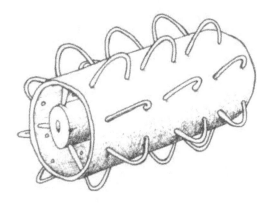

Wire loop thresher

Axial flow engine thresher

of the drum passes along the drum as it is rotated and is ejected at the other end.

Engine-powered threshers may be driven by a small engine mounted on the machine (2hp upwards), or by a tractor. Most machines allow adjustments for various crop and field conditions and a large selection is available with varying drum, power supply, and winnowing/cleaning arrangements. The simplest consist of little more than the threshing cylinder and concave mounted on a framework and include feeding chute, outlets, and a suitable engine.

Winnowing

Various types of machines have been designed to assist the winnowing process. The simplest are essentially hand- or pedal-operated fans with several rotating wooden blades. Slightly more sophisticated are fanning mills, where the fan is mounted in a wooden house which contains sieves and screens. The grain is

thus graded as well as cleaned. The fan may be manually or motor-powered.

Fanning mills produce a very clean product but cannot cope with large amounts of straw, so they are more appropriate for final winnowing. Hand-operated fans are most appropriate for the small-scale farmer.

Maize shelling

There are several types of maize shellers available, ranging from hand-held to manual/pedal- and power-driven ones. Although hand-held shellers are cheap, they have low throughputs and are normally only suitable for small quantities.

Manual/pedal-driven maize shellers consist of a feeder funnel and a shelling disc which is rotated by a crank. The grain is removed as the cob is drawn down through the machine. The output of this type of sheller ranges between 30 and 150kg of grain per hour. Local manufacturers can often supply these.

Engine-powered shellers operate similarly to threshers, with rotating cylinders of the peg or bar type and metal concaves. Cobs must be husked before entering the shelling drum. Some maize shellers have husking rollers which husk the cobs before they are passed to the shelling drum. Engine-powered shellers are not suitable for individual small-scale farmers.

Drying

Traditional methods of drying and storage have developed to take into account local environmental conditions. Before any consideration is given to an improved grain drying or storage system, it is essential first to study the traditional methods used in order to understand their shortcomings (if any), and therefore the need for improved techniques, and second to determine what simple, effective improvements are possible. The traditional methods of drying and storage described in the previous section are simply examples, and in every situation consideration must be given to local traditional methods. Building on what people already know and understand is a sound strategy.

The level of moisture in harvested grain depends mostly on the time of the harvest – obviously, grain harvested in the rainy season will contain more moisture than grain harvested in dry, sunny weather. It is important to note that some grains must contain more moisture than others when harvested if they are to be harvested intact without damage. Both maize and rice can be harvested when the moisture content in the kernels is of the order of 20 per cent (FAO, 1970), although maize can be left in the field to dry further before harvesting. Rice, on the other hand, must not be allowed to dry in the field, or many

of the grains will shatter or fall off the stalks.

It is useful for a farmer to know that drying continues only as long as the air around the grain is able to absorb more moisture from it. If the air contains a lot of moisture, the grain is likely to take in moisture from the air. The farmer should understand this fact because it explains the need to keep dry grain away from moisture or moist air. Grain that is not sealed in a closed container will continue to exchange moisture with the air. During the rainy season, for example, grain will take up moisture if left in an open container. In the hot, dry season, grain will lose the moisture again. (Peace Corps/VITA, 1977).

Grain put into storage should not have more than a certain amount of moisture inside its kernels. The level of moisture for safe grain storage depends, to some extent, upon local conditions. Although the amount of moisture grain can safely hold in storage can change, depending upon storage conditions, some general guidelines for safe moisture contents have been established, as shown in Table 2 (FAO, 1970).

Table 2. Safe moisture contents

Grain type	Maximum moisture content(%)*
Wheat	13.5
Maize	13.5
Paddy	15
Milled rice	13
Sorghum	13.5
Millet	16
Beans	15
Cow peas	15

* (for up to one year's storage at 70% relative humidity and 27°C)

In developing countries, the methods available to farmers for drying crops are usually limited to a combination of sun- and air-drying, although supplementary heat is frequently employed. Drying by a combination of sun and air is often referred to as natural drying.

In all drying, care must be taken to avoid too-rapid drying or over-drying and to minimize excessive movement of the grains which can cause breakage or damage to the seed coat. Over-drying – which can easily occur in arid regions or after excessive exposure to sun or other heat – can cause breakage of the grain, damage to the seed coat, bleaching, scorching, discoloration, loss of germinative power, and nutritional changes. Too-rapid drying of crops with high moisture content can also cause 'case hardening' where the surface of the grain traps moisture within the inner layers (FAO, 1970).

Slow drying, a problem in humid regions, results in the growth of fungi and bacteria, the danger of the grains germinating, and increased losses to predators. In extreme cases this can lead to total loss.

Solar drying is receiving attention because of its low running costs in comparison with traditional fuels. However, the fundamental problem with solar devices is that they do not operate effectively when they are most needed – during a wet spell or during the rainy season. Drying is often complicated by the introduction of high-yield varieties which mature and must be harvested during wet seasons, or by the production of a second, irrigated crop ('double cropping') which must also be harvested during the rains. In these cases the grain requires artificial drying.

Artificial drying involves either the use of air at ambient temperatures and a mechanical means of moving it through the grain, or air heated above ambient temperature with or without the mechanical means of moving it through the produce. Artificial methods include the use of fires to heat the grain directly or indirectly, with or without ventilation. Commercial driers, in which the air is heated by furnaces using oil, the waste heat of an internal combustion engine, or crop residues such as rice husk are also available. Mechanical driers are more appropriate to co-operatives and for service drying by small mills.

Storage

The wide variety of storage techniques already in use usually depend upon many factors including the quantities to be stored, local construction materials and climate. Many of these traditional methods are appropriate and may be used as a basis for improved storage techniques, or continued as methods for storage of the limited amount of grain that is to be used as seed for planting.

Many traditional techniques, such as storage in clay pots which are adequate for very small quantities, cannot be adapted to the storage of larger amounts of grain. As the scale of production increases so that grain can be sold on the market, storage techniques also have to change.

To a considerable degree good storage is a matter of good housekeeping, of paying attention to stored material and recognizing problems before they become too serious. The air between the grains in a store is in equilibrium with the moisture in the grain. Heating and cooling of the store cause this equilibrium to change and this often results in damp layers at the top and bottom of the store. High moisture levels cause the grain to respire at a greater rate and give off heat. Any insect larvae and moulds also begin to grow and reproduce, again giving off heat, and so hot spots occur in the store. If temperatures rise too high, insects migrate to cooler areas causing new trouble spots (Peace Corps/VITA, 1977).

The following points represent a suggested code of good storage practice, and thus offer a set of guidelines in the adoption of an appropriate storage system (Dichter, 1978).

1. Dry grain well before putting it in storage. The grain must then be kept dry.
2. Put only clean grain into containers which themselves have had all old grain, dust, straw, and insects removed and burned, because they could recontaminate the new crop.
3. Keep the grain cool and protect it from large changes in outside temperatures. This can be done in a number of ways: by using building materials (e.g. brick, mud, clay, wood) which do not easily pass on changes in outside temperatures to the stored grain; by keeping or building storage containers away from direct sunlight; or by applying a coat of white plaster to the outside of the containers.
4. Protect the grain from insects by following the rules for cleanliness and drying and by putting the grain into an insect-proof store.
5. Waterproof the buildings and containers as much as possible, preferably when the building is constructed. Storage buildings should be built in well-drained locations and not where they will be flooded by groundwater runoff during heavy rains. This can be achieved by raising the floor of the building off the ground.
6. Make sure containers are rodent-proof in all possible ways.
7. Check the grain regularly while it is in storage to make sure it is not infested. Put your hand into the grain to check for heating, smell the grain, and look for dark kernels (signs of mould), which indicate that the moisture content is rising. If these signs are found, the grain should be tipped out and dried again.
8. Provided they are used in accordance with the manufacturer's recommendations and conform to local government regulations, insecticides mixed into the grain prior to storage may be used to control infestation. *Proper advice must be sought* (Golob, 1977).

Milling, grinding and hulling

There are two basic ways of milling: wet and dry. The latter, as covered in this section, covers the production of cereal flours, mainly from wheat, maize, sorghum and millet. Rice flour is less common in Africa.

Three forces are involved in milling: rubbing (abrasion or shear); impact (hitting with a hammer); and compression (squeezing). All three are always present to some extent, but different types of mill use one force more than the other two. Different materials break in different ways and therefore some mills are better suited to particular cereals.

Conditioning of grain to the correct moisture content prior to milling is important for good separation of the constituent parts. If grain is too dry it is hard, difficult to break down, and requires more energy to convert it to flour. If grain is too moist, material tends to /adhere to machine surfaces and prevent efficient screening. In both cases flour yields and quality are affected.

There is no hard and fast rule for the optimum moisture content of the grain for milling. It will vary with the type of cereal and the particular mill being used. In any case only the larger commercial mills have facilities for moisture measurement. A simple method for assessing whether grain is correctly conditioned is to place a few grains on a hard surface and tap them with a stone. It does not take long to acquire the skill of assessing whether the grain is too hard or too soft.

Dry grain can be conditioned by soaking in water or by leaving it to stand in a closed container with a small amount of water added. Moist grain can be dried by the most convenient method available locally.

There are improved methods of milling, both manual and power-driven. The mills discussed first are stone, plate, hammer and roller mills, followed by hullers used for sorghum/millet and rice. Milling and hulling (sometimes known as dehulling) are two separate functions and are presented as such. It must be stressed from the beginning that in some countries mills are readily available and locally produced while it may be more difficult to obtain them in other areas.

Stone mills

Grinding grains to flour between two flat stone surfaces is the simplest, and must have been the earliest, form of milling. Hand-turned stone mills, sometimes known as querns, consist of a stationary circular base stone, over which a second stone is turned. The grain is fed through the centre of the top stone and is crushed and ground as it moves between the stones towards the periphery. Larger stone mills, which are often of local manufacture, are turned by animal or water power. Stone mills are also commonly turned by diesel or electric motors. This type of mill will produce not only coarse meal but finer flours which are difficult to obtain using other small-scale milling techniques. Small commercial stone mills

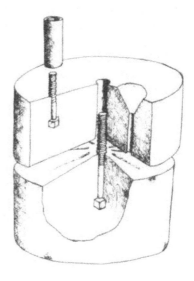

Stone mill (quern)

are available from several countries and stones may be set horizontally or vertically. The most important consideration is the quality of the stone and the precision of the surface dressing.

Plate mills

Plate mills are an adaptation of traditional grinding stones, which grind the grain by a constant rubbing action. In such a mill, two metal plates are mounted on a horizontal axis so that one or both of the plates rotates and the grain is ground between them. The pressure between the plates governs the fineness of the product and is adjusted by a hand-screw. The grain is ground progressively finer until it emerges and falls into a sack or bowl. The main wearing parts are the plates. If a foundry is available, the plates can be made locally.

Plate mills are very effective for wet grinding products such as maize. Water may be added by simply pouring it into the feed section as required. Many manual plate mills are available but the work tends to be hard and throughputs are low, generally less than 10kg per hour. They are however more effective than pounding or grinding stones and will produce a fine meal. If the grain is milled wet it should be cooked as soon as possible.

Power-driven mills are also available. Some of the hand-mills may be fitted with small motors of up to 1hp, so increasing their output and reducing the amount of labour required. Larger units driven by diesel or electric motors of 3hp or more are commercially available.

Hammer mills

Hammer mills essentially consist of a circular chamber in which fixed or swinging hammers rotate at high speed, so grinding the product. The ground material passes through a removable sieve at the base of the chamber into a sack or may be sucked by a fan to an elevated delivery point. The mesh of the sieve plate determines the particle size; a 1mm hole size is suitable for most human foods, whereas a 3mm hole is preferred for animal feed.

The hammers in the mill should be made of hardened steel. Hammers made of soft steel do not last long. Good hammers can be made from lorry/Land Rover leaf springs. They should be replaced approximately every three months, depending on the amount of use. Each hammer can be reversed, so providing a new working surface.

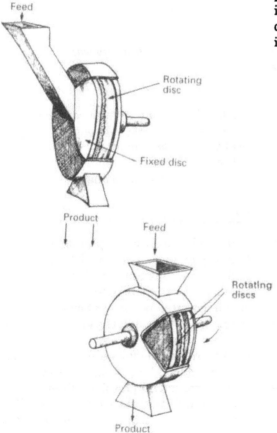

Plate mill

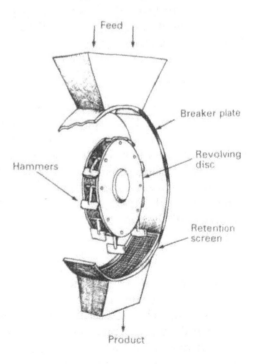

Hammer mill

Both hammer mills and plate mills are equally suitable for dry grinding and it is a matter of cost, availability, product type, and tradition which will decide which mill is used. Hammer mills are easier to operate by unskilled labour and useful for custom milling. Once set up they can be used for long periods without need for adjustment and can produce a uniform product. Hammer mills cannot be used to grind wet grains.

Roller mills

A roller mill consists of a pair of rollers that revolve towards each other, usually at slightly different speeds so producing a shearing force. One roller is held in a fixed bearing, the other has an adjustable spring-loaded bearing so that the gap, and hence fineness of grind, can be adjusted. Roller mills usually operate in series, each producing a finer grade of flour. There is separation of the constituents at each stage. While some small roller mills are available, the technology is usually too sophisticated and expensive for village level operation and is found mostly in urban areas for wheat and maize flour production. The discarded bran and germ are often used for animal feed (ILO/JASPA, 1981).

Huller: sorghum/millet

Improvements in sorghum/millet processing involve two stages which use a huller and a hammer mill. The huller is used to remove the bran from the sorghum before it is milled and it is therefore the key element of the milling system. Abrasive discs or stones set on a horizontal shaft rotate at high speed inside a casing. The hulls are 'rubbed' off by the grinding

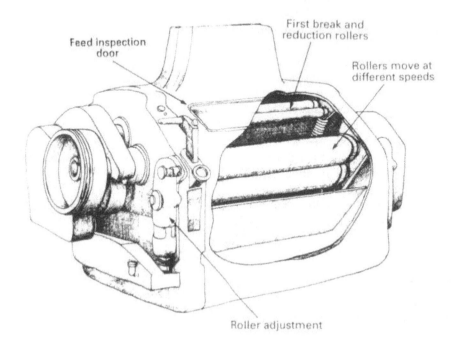

Roller mill

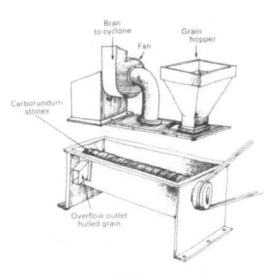

Huller

The under-runner disc husker, which has been used in Asia and some parts of Africa for a long time, consists of two discs, the lower one stationary and the upper rotating. Paddy grains are fed into a central opening in the upper rotating disc and the husk is removed by friction between the two surfaces. In their simplest form the discs are made of clay mixed with water and dried in the sun. Winnowing must again be carried out after this process to separate the kernels from the husk.

The other two machines work on the principle that if a paddy grain is pressed between two resilient surfaces, moving at different speeds in the same direction, to produce a shearing action, the husk will be stripped off. The Engleberg type polishes the rice and removes the husks; in the rubber-roller design polishing is carried out by a separate machine (Mphuru, 1982).

Rubber-roller mills are becoming increasingly popular for several reasons. The use of rubber rollers reduces the risk of breaking the grain and also reduces the

action of the whirling stones and the friction of other grains. The rate of flow of the grain must be adjusted so that the grain is kept in the casing just long enough to remove the desired amount of bran. The lighter bran is continually removed from the hulled grain by a fan. A huller requires a motor with a minimum capacity of 7–10hp (Whitby, 1985).

The hulled grain may be used whole as a rice substitute or ground to a flour or meal in a separate mill. This method of processing sorghum is referred to as 'dry abrasion', because unlike traditional processing it does not use water at any stage of processing.

Rice hullers

There are basically three types of rice huller; a modified version of the under-runner disc husker, the Engleberg steel roller type, and the Japanese rubber-roller.

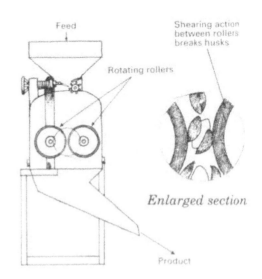

Enlarged section

Rice huller

damage to the machine by unskilled operators. They tend to work better with short grain varieties than with long grain rice. Rubber-roller mills are mechanically efficient but the rollers have to be replaced periodically and may be difficult to obtain. The steel-roller Engleberg mill is more robust, has fewer maintenance problems and usually lasts for many years. However, it causes more grain damage and so reduces quality. This may be important in particular village applications.

It is important to remember that rice polishers remove bran and thus a high proportion of nutrients, particularly B-group vitamins. This may lead to dietary deficiencies in the many areas of the world where rice is a staple food.

Economic considerations

When investing in an improved process, it is important to see whether the improvement will pay for itself. This usually means that the process must earn or save more money than it cost, but not necessarily.

It may be possible for processes to be improved without investing in new machines. If improvements can be made without financial cost, then they are likely to be adopted quickly as long as the perceived benefits to the user outweigh any non-financial costs. These costs could be, for example, having to work in a group rather than working at home, a loss of independence, a loss of control over time allocation in the household. These should not be underestimated, as they can often lead to the abandonment of 'improved' practices.

If, as is more often the case, an improved process requires a level of financial investment, then it is important that the investment produces higher income/quality as well as meeting those other non-financial costs. With crop processing, it is especially important to estimate how many days in the year the machines will be in use. Machines that can be adapted for different crops or processes are likely to be better than machines designed for one job.

Availability of skilled mechanics to maintain the machines, availability of spare parts, and the availability and cost of power (e.g. human, animal, or mechanical) can all have serious impact on the economic viability of an improved process.

If the improved process requires credit, it is important that it will pay for itself and repay the credit as well. Great attention should be paid to the rates of interest available from local institutions and not simply the national bank rate, as these can vary widely.

3
Secondary processing — cereal-based foods

AFTER PRIMARY PROCESSING, cereal products, flour or whole grains are further processed in the home and by small cottage industries into final products. Common final products include foods with a porridge or dough consistency, baked products, whole grain goods, pasta and noodles, fermented drinks, snack foods, and weaning foods. Cereal-based foods are important both for home consumption and as a potential source of income.

Foods with a porridge or dough consistency

Flours from indigenous crops (sorghum, maize, millet, rice) can be mixed and stirred with boiling water to a dough consistency and formed into balls with or without prior fermentation. Foodstuffs such as *banku* and *ugali* made from maize and consumed in Western and Eastern Africa respectively and *sankati* and *tuivo* made from sorghum and consumed in southern India and Nigeria respectively are examples of non-fermented foods. Fermented types such as *kenkey* in Ghana and *bagone* in Botswana are prepared by leaving the whole grain to soak in water for a few days to allow fermentation before grinding to a flour for mixing with water as before. These dough-like cereal foodstuffs provide the basis for a daily meal in many households in Africa.

In India, fermented rice foodstuffs such as *dosais* (rice cakes) and *idlies* (rice pudding) are prepared from a mixture of rice and pulses.

Baked products

Unleavened breads made with maize, wheat or sorghum are popular worldwide as a daily food item. For example, *chapatti* or *roti* are consumed in India, *kisra* in Sudan and *tortillas* in Latin America.

Leavened breads are based on wheat flour and the popularity of these products is in many cases forcing countries to import wheat. Research into composite flour technology (the supplementation of part of the wheat with non-wheat flours) has produced satisfactory bread formulations. It must not be overlooked, however, that such products are not identical to ordinary wheat flour bread and may therefore cause problems of acceptability.

Whole grain foods

Rice is consumed in the tropics mainly as a whole grain, cooked by boiling or frying. Pearled sorghum may be eaten in a similar way, while maize can be roasted or boiled on the cob.

Pasta and noodles

These are popular foodstuffs which are consumed in large amounts and which form the basis of daily meals in many countries. Pasta products require the use of wheat flours but many noodle-like products, such as Sri Lankan *string hoppers*, are based on rice.

Fermented drinks

For many women informal beer production is a very important source of income, but competition from the 'modern' sector with local production has been observed in many areas. It has been shown, in Zimbabwe for example, that as income rises a larger amount of Western or 'modern' beer is consumed to the detriment of local traditional activities. Local brewing, however, is not likely to disappear. Beers can be made from most cereals after they have been 'malted' or allowed to germinate. Examples include sorghum beer, rice wine and maize beers.

Snack foods

A wide range of snack foods can be made by extruding a flour paste into strands (e.g. vermicelli) curls or flakes, by popping (as in puffed rice or popped corn) or by drying to thin sheets (e.g. *papads*). Flavoured mixes such as 'Bombay mix' are also popular.

Weaning foods

Simple weaning foods based on cereals blended with other ingredients can be produced on a small scale. Obviously, great attention has to be paid to the composition of the product, avoiding any ingredient that might be toxic or unsafe from the point of view of hygiene. Young children require essential nutrients such as protein, fat, vitamins and minerals in the correct proportions and a blend must satisfy this need. Expert advice should always be sought before considering establishing projects in this area.

4
Case studies

TRADITIONALLY, CROP PROCESSING activities are carried out primarily by women. The techniques they use are labour-intensive and time-consuming, with low productivity. Two categories of women engage in this type of activity: farm women who process their own crops for family consumption; and landless women, or the wives of marginal farmers, who process other people's crops as a way of supplementing family income.

The introduction of crop processing equipment will have varying implications for these different groups. Labour saving equipment may allow farm women to involve themselves in more remunerative kinds of activity (which would help them pay for the machinery), devote more time to child care, or increase productivity in traditional tasks. However, much of the time saved may be diverted into travelling to the mill and standing in queues for long hours, thus reducing possible benefits.

Landless women may find themselves displaced by crop-processing equipment from their only means of earning a living. For example, as one of the case studies points out, the introduction and spread of Engleberg mills in Bangladesh has destroyed millions of part-time jobs for poor women. Given the greater mechanical efficiency of such equipment compared with traditional techniques, it would be difficult to prevent such changes.

In view of the considerable range of technologies for improved traditional processing of cereals, the selection of the most appropriate technology for a given situation requires a careful examination of social, economic, environmental, and cultural factors as well as an analysis of the competitiveness of traditional processing under given conditions. Obviously, women are only willing to accept new technologies which reduce the most arduous aspects while not creating additional tasks, are viable and appropriate to their needs, and do not deprive them of former economic opportunities.

The tools and equipment used to process crops in the traditional way are mainly locally fabricated, by farm families themselves or by rural artisans. Modern machinery, on the other hand, is usually manufactured in urban factories or even overseas. The introduction of such machinery means a decline in demand for the products of rural artisans and a flow of cash away from the rural economy. It also then results in an increased demand for the country's scarce supplies of foreign exchange for imported machines, spare parts and fuels.

In the following case studies, the machines that are found to be appropriate are often those which are made locally (in the country or neighbouring country) with local skills, resources, and equipment. This implies that use of locally manufactured equipment should be encouraged through measures such as the training of rural artisans, the upgrading of technology in rural workshops, and the provision of credit and other support services.

The case studies seek to provide an overview of the experiences gained in introducing improved cereal processing devices and techniques. Given the lack of documentation on the impact of projects introducing the full range of technologies, the case studies cover only two primary processes – hulling and grinding; and two secondary processing activities – baking and preparation of weaning foods.

Hand/pedal-operated mills

Corn mills in the Cameroons

An obvious hardship for women in the Cameroons in the 1960s was the work involved in grinding maize between two stones. It could take an hour or more of monotonous work to produce even a small quantity of flour, and the women's hands were often covered with calluses. It had already been suggested that corn mills might solve this problem and an opportune grant from the Nigerian Ministry of Education made it possible to set up a revolving loan fund to purchase some mills.

There were no appropriate mills on sale in the Cameroons, but some were eventually traced to a manufacturer in England. These mills were of cast iron and virtually unbreakable. Maintenance involved only occasional oiling and the tightening of nuts which work loose, and changing the grinding plates after one or two years which is quite a simple operation.

Initially, the women were afraid of the unknown, so it took considerable persuasion for them to accept a mill as a gift. Finally, a well-respected elderly woman expressed interest and the women reluctantly agreed to a demonstration. The mill, which broke down into a number of separate parts for head loading, was carried to the village and installed in the centre. Maize was poured down the funnel and two women took the handles on either side and pushed but nothing happened. Trial and error eventually disclosed that new maize (which was being used) must first be dried over a fire if it is not to stick between the grinding plates.

Once this was done all was well, but the two women who had been turning the handles had not yet caught the necessary rhythm and were using six times the energy required, pushing against each other. They declared that the work was too hard and the demonstration stopped. In a few days, however, the situation had changed, and several women had become more familiar with the machine. Soon it was in constant use.

The women's boasts coupled with curiosity soon began to bring in sightseers from all over the area and very soon there were requests from other villages to set up corn mill societies there. The members of these societies were expected to pay for their machines, but were given a year in which to raise the money. At first they made a charge every time a woman used the mill, but later it was found to be administratively simpler to charge a fixed sum per head each month. By the end of the year thirty villages had repaid their loans and more mills had been purchased.

The mills served a dual purpose. First, they lightened the labours of women and allowed them to participate in other activities such as literacy classes and soap-making. Second, they acted as 'bait' to attract members to the societies, since anyone who wished to use a mill had to join a corn mill society. (O'Kelly, 1973)

Christian Council of Tanzania hand-mill project

In 1979 the Christian Council of Tanzania (CCT) initiated a project to provide certain villages with one or more examples of manually operated grinding mills. The purpose of the project was to test the technical and social acceptability of such mills and, subject to a positive finding on both counts, to encourage others to consider the manufacturing of the mills in Tanzania. The project was based in the Arusha region.

Under the project the following mills were imported:

o 24 Atlas hand-mills (Model No. 3), 12 of which were distributed in Arusha region and 12 were sent elsewhere.

o 50 Wheeler-brand hand-mills, manufactured in India. Ten of these were distributed in the Arusha region, with the remaining 40 being stored in Dar es Salaam.

o 20 German-made hand-mills, all of which were distributed in the Arusha region.

o 11 pedal-mills developed by the Tropical Development Research Institute (TDRI), UK, some of which were fitted on to bicycles (with a stand support), and some on to locally constructed wooden pedal units.

The German and Indian hand-mills are both operated by a single handle; the Atlas machine is larger and is designed to be used by two people at the same time. The German and Atlas machines have metal grinding plates, while the Indian mill relies on two grinding stones. The bicycle mill is an entirely different mechanism, being more akin to a hammer mill with the single 'hammer' being rotated by the action of the pedals.

Atlas No. 3 mill

This is a large, robustly manufactured plate mill which, according to the manufacturers, has a grinding capacity of 17–20kg of flour per hour.

The performance of the Atlas mill (and all other non-motorized mills) was judged in accordance with the speed at which it produced an acceptably fine maize flour. Because of villagers' experience with motorized mills they expected a machine to deliver such a product immediately (in the sense that the flour should be produced after passing through the mill only once). Judged by this criterion, the Atlas mill did not grind maize satisfactorily.

The process by which flour of an acceptable quality could be acquired was long and tedious (involving several siftings and regrindings) and was not considered an improvement on the traditional method.

With wheat, sorghum, and millet, however, the results were very different. These grains are much smaller and softer and the mills were popular and well-used when grinding these cereals. The machine could produce an acceptably fine flour quickly and immediately (although one village reported milling wheat twice).

It was found that most of the machines had not been maintained since they were distributed. To some extent this may have reflected on the value of the machine to the users, but probably it also indicates a lack of knowledge or ability to look after the machines. For example, one or two machines had been slightly damaged because villagers had not been able to undo the nuts with spanners and had improvised with other tools.

In addition, villagers seemed to have difficulty operating the Atlas No. 3, and particularly in co-ordinating their movements to enable them to use both handles at the same time. Without exception the second handle had been removed from the machine, most people preferring to take turns to do the grinding so that one can rest while the other works.

Wheeler plate mill

It is regrettable that within the context of the CCT grinding mills project there were some cases when machines were allocated to villages to do work for which they were entirely unsuited. The most striking example of this was the distribution of Wheeler machines to maize-growing areas. Because of a misunderstanding between CCT and the sales representative for the manufacturing company, CCT believed that these machines were capable of grinding maize. Subsequently the company informed CCT that this was not the case and that they were designed to grind millet. By the time this information had been received, however, numerous complaints had been received by CCT and a lot of damage had been done.

This could have been avoided if CCT had pre-tested the machine's technical capability, in which case it is highly unlikely that they would have been distributed, since their performance has been very poor, even with grains for which they were designed. When it was found that the machines were not popular for grinding maize, a letter was written to the villagers requesting that the machines (or at least one of them) be returned so that it could be sent to a different area. This caused a lot of bad feeling in the village because the inhabitants had already contributed to the cost of obtaining the machines. They were already disappointed that the machine did not do the job which they believed it would do (i.e. grind maize), and it only made matters worse when the villagers were asked to return one or more of the machines.

These mills were dismissed by villagers as a complete waste of time. The CCT technician spent a long time trying to improve the mills and get them to work. He requested the assistance of other technicians at SIDO, Arusha, but all efforts were unsuccessful.

German-made plate mills

This mill is rather similar to the Atlas mill in that it utilizes two metal grinding plates. It is a slightly smaller machine, however, with only one handle. It is also lighter and less well-constructed and was simply not strong enough to withstand village conditions.

In a few villages, both an Atlas machine and a German mill were installed. In every case the Atlas machine was preferred, since the German mill broke down or fell into disuse whilst the Atlas continued to give good service. The failure of the German mill seems to be connected with the lighter flywheel and handle. In a number of villages the mill had been used quite regularly until the handle broke.

Bicycle and pedal mills

A bicycle mill is, as its name suggests, a mill attached to a bicycle. A pedal mill is one where the bicycle has been replaced by a wooden frame. The following points should be noted about the mills.

o The TDRI mill was originally intended to be used on a bicycle which the villager already owned, so if the villager had no bicycle, she or he could not use the mill. For testing purposes, bicycles were provided. This was unsatisfactory because the men in the village considered grinding maize to be a waste of a good bicycle and they took off the mill and used the bicycle for other purposes. It is significant that pounding grain is women's work and the men clearly could see no value in the bicycle helping the women to do that job.

o Women were generally not prepared to use a bicycle. Traditionally it is men who ride bicycles and village women find it embarrassing to do so. Such is their reluctance to use the bicycle that there were instances when women got down on their knees and turned the pedal by hand.

o An attempt was made to overcome these social problems by introducing a pedal mill attached to a wooden frame made at the Arusha Appropriate Technology Project. This proved unsuccessful because the frame was not strong enough, and was very uncomfortable when pedalling.

○ None of the TDRI mills of either variety is being used now and the villagers seem to have no interest in pursuing this approach. Flour produced by the mill is reasonably good, but output is very low. Once again, maize is the most difficult and requires milling two or three times. Production of a kilo of maize flour takes 2–4 hours.

It was concluded that the TDRI mills were not acceptable for use in Tanzania.

Community Development Trust Fund hand-mills in Tanzania

The daily chore of grinding or pounding the basic food requirements of a family is a major burden for the women of Tanzania. During the 1980s, there was a drive to supply villages with diesel-powered grinding mills. These were provided, frequently on loan terms, because they were considered by a wide range of agencies to be suitable for income-generating projects.

Diesel mills were – and still are – very popular with villagers. The success of the mills, however, depends to a large extent on factors beyond Tanzania's immediate control. In particular, they require substantial amounts of foreign exchange, not only for the initial importation but also for the fuel and spare parts to keep them going. Not surprisingly, then, the severe economic problems of recent years have adversely affected the economic and operational viability of diesel mills. Many hundreds, particularly village-owned mills, are now standing idle or have broken down. Inevitably, the problem is more severe in areas which are geographically isolated and relatively undeveloped economically.

Recognition of the extent of the problems of diesel mills has caused many of the agencies formerly involved in their supply to review the position. Most have reduced the provision of mills and some have put a complete stop on them. Such changes in policy have obvious implications for the thousands of villages in the country which do not yet have a diesel mill. The prospect facing the women of these villages is one of either spending a lot of time and energy walking to and from (and invariably waiting at) the nearest diesel mill or of continuing to use the slow and difficult methods which have not been improved upon for generations. In an attempt to solve this dilemma the hand-mills project was set up by the Community Development Trust Fund (CDTF).

Initially, research was carried out to identify, from a variety of models, a particular type of hand-mill best suited for use in village conditions in Tanzania. Areas for testing the mills were determined by the range of food crops grown, i.e. maize, sorghum, and millet, and the absence of motor mills in a village was one of the factors that determined its selection. It also reflected CDTF's commitment to working directly with the poorer and/or remote villages.

In examining the social acceptability of hand-mills, CDTF was interested in finding out whether or not the villagers preferred them, and also in investigating ways in which the benefits of hand-mills could be enjoyed by all the villagers and not just a minority of them. From the beginning it was recognized that there were financial and social differences between individuals which could affect the general acceptance of hand-mills. Thus, a large part of the work was directed towards searching for and then strengthening an ownership pattern that would enable all sections of the community to participate in and benefit from the project, and a decision was made to encourage communal ownership.

A principal objective of the project was to encourage and facilitate the participation of women. CDTF wanted to prevent the introduction of hand-mills from having a negative effect on women. For example, in the vast majority of diesel mill projects women are reduced to passive recipients of a service which is entirely controlled by men. However, the idea of treating the project as a 'women-only' activity was rejected because of the fear that this would merely emphasize the isolation of women from the mainstream of village (and national) development.

The project was implemented in five villages. The villages selected were divided into two categories: those that had been suggested by others active in the area on the basis of their need/remoteness, and those that had already identified grinding as a problem and had put forward applications for a diesel mill.

In initial village meetings the villagers were given the opportunity to hear for themselves the background to the project, its purpose and duration, and what would be their rights and responsibilities in conducting the trials. Models of the hand-mills were displayed and short demonstrations were given on how to use them. After a long question and answer session the villagers were asked to decide whether or not they wanted to take part in the project.

The next meeting, held at the co-operative group level, was to decide at which homesteads the mills would be installed. At this level, the interest of the villagers was very high and attendance at meetings was good.

During these meetings it was emphasized that selection of a household did not mean the mill would become the property of that household – rather, that the mill was the property of co-operatives and was being placed with one of their members in trust for use by all. While every member had a right to use the mill, they were also reminded that they had a joint responsibility to build a shelter for it, look after it, and prevent its misuse.

The mills were set up outside the home, so as to facilitate easy access by all with a minimum amount of disturbance to the householder. Installation was carried out by the villagers. CDTF remained in the village for one week after installation for intensive supervision. Because the mill was new and the villagers inexperienced in using it, a great deal of attention had to be given to providing training on usage and maintenance. In particular, it was essential that they became familiar with the purpose of the grinding regulator, which controls the fineness of the grain and the energy required to operate the mill. Frequent guidance was necessary on how and why to adjust the regulator.

Within a few days of installation a second meeting was called to discuss the issue of maintenance. There was a need for villagers to develop the habit, as well as to acquire the skills, of looking after the mill, for even a simple machine like a hand-mill requires regular attention, cleaning, greasing, and so on. Unless specific individuals are given these tasks there is a danger that each user will leave them to someone else until the machine breaks down. An unpaid maintenance team of two women and one man was selected by the group from among their number. A day of intensive instruction was given to the three people concerned, each in turn learning to take apart and then reassemble the mill.

The hand-mills were on trial for four to six months. At the end of that period a further village assembly was held to decide which, if any, of the hand-mills were satisfactory and whether to take up the option of buying some or all of them. Much still remained to be done, including decisions on the ownership pattern to be followed in the future, how future mills would be paid for, and what form of system should be adopted to pay for spare parts and ensure their supply. Although the village, as an institution, accepted this responsibility in the trials stage, when the number of mills was small and therefore easy to look after, it is doubtful whether it will be the most suitable implementing authority as the project grows. Alternative or supplementary structures are needed and it is the process of identifying them and making them function that is the next challenge.

Diesel/electric powered mills

Community Development Foundation corn mills in Honduras

South Honduras is the most impoverished area in one of the poorest countries in the western hemisphere. Three-quarters of the rural population hold a mere one-tenth of all cultivated land. Over 70 per cent live in settlements of less than 2000 people.

When the Community Development Foundation (CDF) came to the remote village of Esquimay, they found it situated on a plateau, surrounded by dry, hilly terrain that afforded one harvest a year of sorghum, beans, and corn. Vegetable gardening simply did not exist. Men would return from long, hot hours in the fields listless and exhausted.

The primary source of income for Esquimay was the sale of rosquillas, hard biscuits made from corn and cheese. Women would have to rise at four in the morning to grind the corn and prepare the dough. Grinding alone would consume such a tremendous amount of time that the supply could only satisfy part of the demand, which was in the hills and towns, some of them 17 kilometres away. The women did all the marketing themselves, making the long journey only after they had baked enough rosquillas.

CDF assistance had been requested by a housewives' club, who had heard that the agency was working with other villages in the area. After hearing a description of the village's economic situation, CDF staff surmised that the community might identify its key development issue as increased income through better rosquilla production. However, they realized that first the whole community, men and women together, would have to see itself as an economic unit, then it could realize its potential as a decision-making unit and collaborate on economic objectives and plans of action. A community meeting in the village church was called at CDF's request to determine how this process would best work. As expected, the men were somewhat resentful of women being included, but they seemed to accept it provisionally, probably because they realized that it was a housewives' club that had invited CDF there, and because they were interested in what would happen. CDF staff saw that for both men and women this was to be a strange, new bilateral planning process, and that it would be thoughtful but not excessive guidance that would put people at ease with it.

The community was asked to identify their first development objective and their reply was not what the planners had expected. They said that they wanted to build a new school for their children, because the building they had was in a poor condition. This might have been what they thought a voluntary agency would like to hear, that their prime concern was making their children happy through education and that education superseded all other priorities in their minds. Nevertheless, CDF planners were not there to reject their priorities, but to get the community to think systematically through its conclusions, and evaluate them in terms of maximum community benefit. Will this money for a school building replenish itself? No, it disappears when spent. Then how would you raise that much money if you were to finance this project yourselves? Through an exploratory discussion they revealed that their only source of income came through the sale of rosquillas and that they had a good market but poor production capacity. Now they were considering means of increasing output to augment their income.

However, before CDF would discuss any labour-saving technology, the community had to identify the major obstacle to full production, and for this the women's role had to be considered carefully. In addition to producing and selling rosquillas, women were responsible for household duties and for caring for their children. Washing clothes and drawing water were endless chores, especially when coupled with the steep climb from the stream back to the village. It was becoming apparent to the community that these responsibilities in themselves were very extensive and that when combined with the rosquilla trade they left the women no free time. How would increased corn production through intermediate farming technology boost rosquilla output when women were already overloaded with work? It was obvious that any labour-saving device would have to alleviate the women's hardship.

The community reasoned that the long hours required to grind the corn caused the most severe strain and was also the major obstacle to increased production. CDF therefore donated the down payment and made a loan of the first instalment for the motor-driven mill which grinds corn in a matter of seconds. Women pay the mill operator a small fee per kilo, which is deposited in the community treasury. Budgeting with CDF, the community estimated that the $1000 cost could be repaid within a year and a half. In fact, the treasury would have sufficient funds for a new mill long before the end of the first mill's ten-year life span.

The accounts show that rosquilla production exceeds 10 000 per day. Women's work in this area has decreased appreciably, and they are free to become involved in other activities of their own choosing. Furthermore, the process of selecting appropriate small technology and operating it for the common benefit greatly increased this village's initiative in planning other endeavours. For instance, at community request, the president and other members of the committee built an extension to the community centre. With CDF assistance, they began a small co-operative store within it. The construction work was completed without remuneration and all store profits are deposited in a community fund which exists in part to pay for the children's education.

The villagers are well aware of the fact that CDF's presence could, for any number of reasons, terminate in the near future. However, the improvements that the community has implemented on its own behalf have given it confidence in its own planning capabilities.

Some will say that sex roles have not undergone revolutionary changes here, but the people recognize that both men and women share an economic stake in the improvement of their lives and they know that there must be communication between them before any planning can occur. Through their own assessment, the people have seen that the roles of men and women must be equalized, both in workload and in decision-making authority. They know that as a community they have not only hope for but influence over their children's future. (Fennelly Levy, undated)

Women's mill organization, Senegal

In Senegal, large amounts of grain are traditionally threshed by a work group or *santanée*. The village women respond to an invitation to help thresh one woman's grain and bring a tubful or two of their own millet to be threshed at the same time. The santanée usually continues all day, with some women coming and going as their other responsibilities require. Payment to the threshers includes a midday meal and the assurance that they will also be able to recruit help when they have a large threshing task.

With the arrival of the thresher, huller, and mill in one project village, the threshing of the family's grain became the realm and financial responsibility of the men. This is probably because of the heavy work involved in bringing bundles of grain heads to be threshed and subsequent handling of the large quantities of threshed grain. The women were the obvious benefactors in this case, being freed both from the manual threshing task and the expense of employing the machine. It is hard to say why the men took the threshing activity upon themselves with the advent of the machines, yet for the most part did not feel their responsibility extended as far as mechanical hulling and milling of millet.

One clue may be in the ease of these tasks. Maize, for example, which could be ground at one time in one large quantity, was taken to the mill and paid for by the men. It is conceivable that most men did not consider the processing of relatively small amounts of millet for daily consumption as a task worthy of their attention, although they would probably pay for processing any millet specifically destined for sale. Men usually sell millet in the form of threshed grain (*dougoub*), and once they have paid for mechanical threshing for their entire crop, they are free to sell it as they wish.

Users of the mechanical grinder for millet fell into two general categories: regular and irregular users. Paying for the services of the grinder was in many households the wife's responsibility: if she had some cash, she would have that day's millet ground by machine, if not, she would pound. These women were the irregular users. Women whose husbands paid for the use of the grinder were the regular users and pounded only on days that the mill was not in operation, chiefly Saturday afternoon and Sunday. Probably the most significant factor in determining which women were frequent users of the grinder was whether or not the husband paid.

Many women brought their grain to the centrally located mill on their way to perform some other task, such as drawing water, and returned later to pick up the flour. It is interesting to note that some received more and some less than their due of flour. This was because the women brought their grain to the miller wet and the moisture caused some of the flour to stick in the machine. Then, when this flour dried somewhat, it became dislodged and came out of the machine along with the grain currently being processed, which might have been several bowls later. This woman would receive more flour than she should. The miller asked the women to allow the grain to dry before bringing it to the mill, so as to reduce the sticking problem. The women generally did not comply, however, because they moistened the grain for hulling so as to produce a cleaner product, and then brought it to the mill in whatever condition when they wanted it ground. Perhaps they recognized that even if they lost some grain on one day they might gain some the next day.

It was found that very few women used the huller because they found it too expensive. Most women could afford either hulling or milling. Women preferred to pay for machine milling rather than hulling because milling by hand was much more time-consuming and tiring than hulling by hand. They also found that the machine produced more broken grains than hand hulling. Machine hulling and milling resulted in a product of lower quality, containing more bran, than the flour produced by hand hulling and subsequent machine (or hand) milling.

Many of the women interviewed stressed the low quality of the product produced by the huller. They claimed it left too much bran in the flour and some women who used the huller pounded the grain slightly with water after machine hulling and winnowed it to remove the remaining bran. Some women also complained that the huller broke too many grains, presumably a problem if the women wanted to pound and winnow the grain again by hand before grinding. (Loose, 1979)

Diesel mills and women's education, Burkina Faso

The Upper Volta (Burkina Faso)/UNESCO/ UNDP Women's Education Project, an informal education programme, launched as long ago as 1967, is as relevant today as it was in the 1970s, mainly because its long duration allowed a thorough evaluation of its objectives and achievements. In addition, the technologies introduced by the project tackled the three work areas which were then and still are the most burdensome for rural women in the South: crop processing, collecting and carrying water, and gathering fuelwood.

Following the failure of many formal education projects introduced to try to involve rural women in significant numbers, the informal Women's Education Project was launched with two main ob-

jectives: to gather data on the barriers preventing the full access of women to education and to initiate experimental programmes to overcome these obstacles. As well as addressing the issue of women's excessive workloads, the project also tackled the problems of poor health and low standards of living: all factors which preliminary sociological studies had pinpointed as fundamental problems.

Three labour-saving technologies were introduced, with the idea that the time saved through using these could be devoted to training the women in improved agricultural methods, health and civic education, income-generating activities, and literacy. Dynamic village women and traditional midwives were chosen by the villagers to attend special training courses in knowledge dissemination. Each village association organized by these women was given a mechanical grain-grinding mill and carts for the transportation of wood, water, and crops; easily accessible wells were dug, too. The plan was for the village women to use the equipment on their own behalf, but to have the opportunity to rent it out in order to earn revenue for the co-operative.

From 1976 to 1979 an evaluation of the project was carried out to establish whether lack of time did, in fact, constitute a significant barrier to educational activities; to determine the effectiveness of the appropriate technologies introduced; and to assess how far the project had increased the participation of women and girls in education programmes. The conclusion was that women worked longer hours than their husbands, averaging over twice as much time on production, supply and distribution tasks, including food processing, and they spent twice as much time on these activities as on the household tasks of cooking, cleaning, washing, and child care. With only 1.3 hours of free time in the women's first

14 waking hours, it is little wonder that the project team gave priority to the introduction of technologies to lighten workloads.

The grinding/pounding activity absorbs some 84 per cent of total food processing time or an average of more than 1.75 hours a day. Following the introduction of mechanical mills, it was discovered that 14 of a sample of 30 women in the village used the mills to grind their grain. Lack of money was the most frequent reason given for non-use, even though the fee for operating the mills was usually fixed by the women's group and was nominal in comparison with prevailing commercial prices.

The mills were portable and fitted with a 4.5hp motor. On average, they were grinding 5–12kg of grain per hour, 54–90kg per day. All the mills were at the disposal of the women, and the people designated to look after them were either chosen by the women or were the women themselves, except in two villages where they were kept by the sons of the chief. The mills seemed to reduce the time spent on pounding and grinding activities, and although the time saved tended to be used to do other household tasks, the decision to introduce mechanical mills to reduce the time taken to process grain was clearly a sound one. However, in 1978, six years after the introduction of ten mills in the Kongoussi zone, only five were in working order. Breakdowns were mainly the result of inadequate maintenance, such as forgetting to put oil in the motor. Rural mechanics were subsequently trained to maintain the mills. But unfortunately, the delays encountered in acquiring spare parts are still a problem, not to mention the cost of spare parts themselves. Whereas the government had moved, in collaboration with ILO/UNDP, in favour of local production of ploughs, similar results concerning the local pro-duction of mills had yet to be achieved. Meanwhile, project personnel were ever on the lookout for less sophisticated devices. (McSweeney, 1982)

Mechanized rice hullers, Indonesia

On governmental initiative, mechanized rice hullers were introduced in Indonesia in 1970–71. The diffusion of hullers occurred very rapidly after 1970, and by 1978 only about 10 per cent of paddy was being hand-pounded, mostly for family consumption.

A Japanese model that uses rubber rollers is common in Indonesia. Pasawahan, a village in West Java, has three milling centres that use Japanese hullers and polishers. Rice must be processed through the machine four to eight times. It is first poured into the top of the huller; the hulls and excess material (bran) then travel through a pipe and are discarded outside the building. The hulled rice is then run through the polisher three or four times.

The mill has taken over work traditionally done by women: two examples illustrate these changes. A former rice trader, now turned mill owner, stated that he used to employ eight women to hand-pound his rice. Four women working five hours could hand-pound 100kg of gabah. This rice trader could buy 200kg per day of gabah. The women's wages were 10 per cent of the rice they provided, which amounted to just under two litres of milled rice per day. Thus, over the harvest season these eight women earned perhaps 60 litres of milled rice each, or enough to feed themselves for four months. In Kendal, Central Java, a farmer said that in the past there were more than one hundred women hand-pounders in his village. Now they have no work.

Estimates of jobs lost range as high as 1.2 million in Java alone and as high as 7.7 million in all of Indonesia as a result of the introduction of the new technology. It is estimated that the loss to labourers in earnings because of the use of hullers was US$50 million annually in Java, representing 125 million days of labour.

The rice farmer pays less to the mill and the process is much quicker, but the women are now forced to work longer hours at other jobs, if such work can even be found. The shift from a traditional technology to a more modern one has eliminated one of the more important sources of income for landless villagers. Thus, although the adoption of the use of high-yield varieties, tebasan, sickles, scales and rice hullers has served to increase rice production in Indonesia, it has not helped to solve problems of unemployment and uneven income distribution in Java. Rather, it appears these problems have been exacerbated. Furthermore, there is little evidence to indicate that the rural unemployed are being taken up by work opportunities in the cities, or have been able to find replacement sources of income in the rural areas. (Cain, 1981)

Rural rice hullers, Bangladesh

The most significant impact of the spread of rural rice hullers in Bangladesh is the effect they have had on employment. The average rural huller has a capacity of 160 maunds per day (1 maund = 37.3kg) as opposed to the traditional manual rice huller or *dheki's* capacity of 1.3 maunds per day. This means that every mill (if working at capacity) displaces 123 dhekis, each of which provided part-time employment to two or three women operators. A significant number of women have lost a traditional source of productive part-time employment as a result.

Three different categories of women are involved in the milling process. First, there are the female members of large-surplus farms. In general, they have benefited from the change in technology since although they did not have to do dheki work themselves, they had to supervise hired labour. If they now use the mill they have more leisure time and their families have benefited economically, as husking by rice mill is cheaper than paying dheki labour. Second, there are female members of subsistence farms who previously had to do dheki work themselves if they did not use a rice mill; they too will have benefited since they will have been relieved from a time-consuming and physically demanding task. Their level of mill use will, however, be restricted by their ability to pay cash for milling, and in some cases transportation costs. Third, there are wage-labour women from landless families who do dheki work to augment family income. The lack of alternative sources of equally remunerative employment means that these women and their families have suffered badly in the absence of initiatives aimed at helping them to cope with the introduction of new competitive technologies.

One way of assisting such women is to find income-generating activities other than rice hulling for them. Another is to help the women control and exploit the technology rather than letting it exploit them. One example of the latter response is the Purba Pol Mogra Women's Association rice husking mill which was set up with a Grameen Bank (GB) loan in 1982.

For some time, Nurjahan Begum had cherished the idea of initiating a joint enterprise. She attended several workshops and discussed the issue with other borrowers and GB workers. When she went to the Madhupur Workshop, she was inspired by the success story of the Narandia Women's Association which had just set up the first all women rice husking mill, and she started a campaign in her own area in favour of setting up a similar enterprise.

During the first few weeks of her campaign, most of the group members considered it was an impractical proposition, but later they were convinced. Grameen Bank workers also stressed the importance of group-based activities and the idea gained more and more support. Forty women divided into eight groups contracted a loan from the GB to set up a husking machine.

The machine was installed in a cow shed in the yard of Nurjahan's house. The group members made another shed for Nurjahan's cattle, and they all joined in setting up the machine house. They themselves supplied the necessary materials for the construction of the shed except for bamboo and corrugated iron sheets, which they bought with a loan from their group fund. They broke about 50 maunds (three tonnes) of rock into small pebbles for flooring.

Nurjahan trained herself to operate the machine and in turn taught other members. There is an eight-member committee to manage the rice mill. Ordinary members participate in cleaning the machine house and changing the water of the reservoir. Nurjahan and her companions are very eager to eliminate dependence on others for running the machine; she has already attained some proficiency in operating the machinery and has also recruited apprentices.

The machine uses diesel fuel. One gallon of diesel is needed to husk 20–25 aari of paddy (1 aari is approx. 15kg). The rate they charge for husking has been fixed according to the price of diesel and the existing market rate. Several aaris of paddy are collected before the machine is started; so far the highest daily husking stands at 67 aaris.

Since the setting up of the husking machine, trade in paddy has received a boost in the neighbourhood. At present, there are four women who are full-time rice traders and their income has increased. Local men have also started to come to husk their rice in this machine when their machine in the market place becomes inoperative because of electricity failure. As this happens very frequently, the demand for Nurjahan's machine is increasing steadily.

Many of those who opposed the setting up of the mill in the beginning have now become patrons and clients. People come from far away to see the women-operated rice mill. It is raising hopes and, though it has not yet attained the break-even point, it is a source of inspiration for others.

To repay the bank loan, about 60–65 aaris of paddy has to be husked every day. The present rate is only about one-third of this, but all the signs are that it is going to be a successful venture. (Scott and Carr, 1985, and Khan, 1982)

Locally manufactured mills, Kenya

In South Nyanza, grinding mills known as 'posho mills' are locally manufactured in Gilgil. All the mills are owned by men and are primarily commercial ventures. A women's group tried to purchase one of the mills but found the cost prohibitive. They tried to get a loan, but most of the women had only just started to have bank accounts and so were still becoming acquainted with handling large sums of money.

Women use the existing mills as service mills because it relieves them of grinding chores. A visit to the mill is a social occasion for them, despite the long walk, as they can meet other women there. As a result, markets have grown up around the mills and people are taking advantage of them to sell their produce. Some of the mills charge high prices, so it is not unusual for women to walk greater distances with heavy loads to reach a less expensive mill. However, with large families, service milling can be very expensive, so women still grind using traditional stones and use the mills only when they have some spare money.

Locally manufactured millet mill, Senegal

In the village of Morry Laye in Senegal, after a harvest that was slightly better than that of previous years, the villagers decided to buy a millet mill. Of course, Morry Laye is not the only village with a mill, but this is a very special one, made (apart from the motor which powers it) by a village craftsman. The locally manufactured millet mill is an improvement over the imported mills installed elsewhere, according to the Morry Laye villagers.

Traditionally, before the millet or sorghum is ground, it is either washed or moistened to trigger fermentation of the grain. This gives food a better taste, especially in the preparation of *lakh* (millet porridge) or *tiere* (couscous).

'You see, imported mills are different from ours' says one of the women in front of the hut housing the millet mill. 'You can't use wet grain in the imported mills. You must always use dry grain and this doesn't give the same taste. Even my husband complained about it – he doesn't like the imported mills. Some women even have to resort to old-fashioned pounding methods because their husbands won't accept the new taste.'

There are other problems with the imported mills; for instance, the sieves may be too small and they may clog, with the result that it takes a tremendous amount of time to mill the grain, and fuel consumption is considerably increased.

'With our mill we have no problems. We use moistened millet and the flour comes out very white and fine. This did not happen with the imported mills, which gave us a kind of paste.' When asked how long it took to pound three kilos of millet in the past, the woman smiles and says: 'With my two daughters helping me, it used to take me two to three hours a day to pound our grain'. Now it takes three minutes.

In addition to the time saved, there are many other advantages. With the traditional system – pounding, winnowing, washing, and pounding again – as much as a third of the grain could be lost. Also, the grain was first separated from the stalk and the latter, although of great nutritional value, was fed to the livestock. With the mill, the stalk is finely milled and eaten with the flour. Local mills can also be used equally well for millet and sorghum and for peanuts and cassava. Different-sized sifters can also produce flour suitable for making couscous. The price of the mill, including installation, the miller's training, and the maintenance of the equipment for twelve months, is less than the cost of an imported mill, and far better adapted to the villagers' real needs. (UNICEF, 1983)

Locally produced sorghum mills, Botswana

In 1975 the Government of Botswana asked the Botswana Agricultural Marketing Board (BAMB) to investigate the mechanical processing of sorghum to relieve the back-breaking, time-consuming toil of many women who spend hours pounding the grain. In co-operation with the International Development Research Centre (IDRC), BAMB installed Botswana's first commercial sorghum mill at Pitsane in 1977 and this was working completely under local management by late 1978.

By making processed sorghum available, the mill regenerated a demand for Botswana's traditional food, which the imported mealie meal (maize) had been replacing. Clearly, even at a cost greater than the mealie meal, the people of Botswana preferred *mabele* (sorghum). The commercial mill was large, however, capable of processing four to five tonnes per day, and it relied on large supplies of sorghum from BAMB, so it was situated on a road and rail network in order to operate efficiently. Realizing this and supported by reports on consumer preferences, the Rural Industries Innovation Centre (RIIC), in further collaboration with IDRC set about designing a smaller and more versatile unit for the varying needs of rural communities who grew their own sorghum.

Between 1978 and 1980 RIIC redesigned, developed, and tested various prototypes of a scaled-down huller. The eventual outcome was a machine, smaller than the Pitsane model, which could operate at high speeds and process the same sort of quantitites. In 1979 the RIIC installed one of their models in their home village of Kanye and later that year another at Pelegano Village Industries in Gabane for trials. A survey in Kanye clearly showed the need for such machines, as did later reports on the sorghum mills placed elsewhere.

A seminar was held in September 1979 for potential investors in the equipment, with RIIC taking orders. A mill owners' handbook and a promotional booklet were produced which described the benefits of an investment in the equipment as well as giving information on how to run a business as a mill owner. The first course for mill owners took place in February 1980 and production of hullers began early that year.

With such rapid development and uptake of a technology, it is not surprising that

there were a few problems with the early machines. A Post-Harvest Technology Programme was set up by RIIC's parent company, Rural Industries Promotion, to investigate claims and counter-claims of incorrect user practices and low quality manufacture. The conclusion was that technical refinements were needed, educational and organizational support for the mill owners and an infrastructure able to provide quick and effective support (such as the supply of spares, repair and maintenance) were also very important. Perhaps more significant, however, was the establishment of the Botswana Mill Owners Association in 1983, for the owners to share a forum of mutual interest.

The RIIC design lends itself to batch service milling as well as continuous commercial milling. The RIIC handbook recommends the combination of service milling in the morning and commercial milling in the afternoon. Thus villagers can either buy sorghum meal or bring their own grain for milling.

Service milling for women means relief from a daily and laborious task, as long as they are able to afford it. A survey in 1981 concluded that the mill could release up to four hours per day of a woman's time. It indicated that this was usefully spent in 'productive' activities such as mixing clay, weeding, knitting, or beer brewing; and the children, who would have helped with the milling, could study or read.

The complete mill comprises a huller to remove the bran, a hammer mill to grind the hulled grain into meal, and a diesel engine. Finance was available from the National Development Bank, the Botswana Government's Financial Assistance Policy, and other sources. The mills are run by co-operatives, brigade centres, and private individuals, providing over 250 jobs.

The credit for this success story is due to the Rural Industries Innovation

Centre, for maintaining the momentum of interest through many changes of personnel over the period of the project. Many other institutions suffer from personnel changes every two or three years and a general lack of interest among new recruits in taking over where someone else left off. In this example, however, it was clear that the technology was well-researched from the basic need, through consumer preference, technology choice and carefully monitored implementation, to the impact of the technology on the people it was designed to help. An indication that RIIC was correct in evaluating technology needs was highlighted in the setting up of the Post-Harvest Technology Programme with continued interest in the technology being demonstrated by the establishment of the Botswana Mill Owners' Association. (Whitby, 1985)

Alternative energy

Solar-powered mill, Burkina Faso

In Tangaye, a village with a population of about 2000 inhabitants, women are responsible for processing grain for the preparation of all food consumed in the village. Grain is ground for domestic use, and for the purposes of brewing beer and baking cakes to be sold in the market.

There are two commercial mills in the vicinity. In a village-wide survey it was reported that almost all families had used commercial mills at one time or another. Approximately 61 per cent of the families used the mills only after 1975, even though they had been there since 1968. The highest frequency of use (55 per cent) occurred during the rainy season. Large quantities of millet, more than 8 litres, were usually ground at this time.

Regular users of the mills were generally vendors who sold produce in the market where the mills are housed. The majority of the residents of Tangaye availed themselves of the mill only on special occasions. However, daily observations at mill sites revealed that more than 90 per cent of the customers using the mill were women, mostly residents of the village in which the mill was housed, coming to grind small quantities of grain for the evening meal. This proved that the services of the mill were still in great demand even for women who did not go to the market as regularly as vendors.

The mills were powered by imported diesel oil, and the price of milling services increased with the rise in fuel cost. As a result of this, the millers lost so many customers that they were forced to open their mills twice a week, on market days, rather than every day as they had done in the past. Few people in the area could afford the increase in milling rates. Buying fuel makes up 50–60 per cent of the monthly budget of running the mill. Clearly an inexpensive source of energy was essential if the residents of the area were to have access to such labour-saving devices.

In 1978, a solar unit or photovoltaic system, the first of its kind, was introduced to the village of Tangaye. The unit consisted of a solar cell array designed to transform solar energy into electricity and a battery designed to store electricity. This photovoltaic system supplies the electricity necessary to power a food grinding capacity of 92kg of sorghum per hour. Millet and maize may also be ground, though at a reduced hourly capacity.

Diet, food preparation, and level of consumption vary significantly from the dry to the rainy season. During the dry season women spend at least 60 per cent of their working day processing food and fetching water. In the rainy season, however, they devote the greater part of their day to farming and thus spend less time on processing food, including occasionally cooking whole grains, rather than making flour, and grinding a coarse rather than a fine flour.

It was established, therefore, that the mill would be a great help to women in the dry season when the volume of food processing was at its height. During the rainy season the presence of a mill might affect the quality of the food consumed rather than contribute to the time saved in processing, especially considering the time taken to travel to the mill and waiting to be served.

A system of managing the mill was devised so that the villagers would be able to invest in it and share in the profits from the services provided. The idea of not charging for the services of the mill was dismissed because of potential conflict and monopolization of resources by a certain segment of the population: it would be impossible to equalize access to the mill without excessive policing.

Those willing to invest in the mill by providing services and the money for the operating costs would have a share of the monthly profit, part of which has to be put aside for future investments in development projects within the village that they themselves decide upon. In this way, it was hoped that private investors and the entire community would benefit from the profits of the milling enterprise.

For a system like this to work, it is necessary to have input from the population. This requires an intensive information programme permitting villagers to criticize the system, detect possible flaws, suggest improvements, or even propose other management plans better suited to their needs. Even before the mill is installed, it is necessary to inform the villagers of the implications of housing such a system in the village. They should

then be asked whether, given the risks, they want it installed. Only then should they decide, knowing the full implications of housing such a unit. The villagers should make all the decisions relating to the organization of labour, the sharing of profits, and so on. Last, but not least, the provision must be made for the maintenance and repair of the mill. Permanent members of the village, particularly those most concerned with the services offered (women and vendors) should be trained in the proper maintenance and repair of the mill and pump. (Hemmings-Gapihan, 1981)

Cereal product businesses

Bomani Baking Co-operative, Kenya

The women of Bomani were challenged by the staff of the informal education project in Kenya to identify the needs in their village, and then to work together to fulfil those needs. The answer, the woman decided, was to start a bakery. They earned the money to get started by selling their traditional handicrafts – *vivywele* and *vivangi* (small baskets and weaving) – through Tototo Home Industries. The women hired help to build the big brick oven. Two members of the group went to Kanamai to learn how to bake bread and returned to train the other women of Bomani. The women elected a treasurer, pooled their money to buy supplies and worked out a schedule for sharing the baking and marketing of the bread.

The bakery turned out to be far more than an activity in economic development for Bomani. Health, nutrition, sanitation, family life, business skills, co-operation between men and women, and leadership in the village were all affected by the women's project.

For a start, the bakery had to be built according to government specifications. A latrine was required by law. The Ministry of Health set standards of cleanliness for workers to follow: workers had to be immunized against certain diseases.

When good bread became available throughout Bomani, the children, who had to walk a long distance to school, had something good and wholesome to carry along for lunch.

The men were impressed by what the women had done and many began to help. Some did so by 'allowing' their wives to go to the training sessions; others contributed money or labour. The women learned to keep records, manage their money, and use the financial services of a bank. Many are learning to read and write and to use more sophisticated mathematics in accounting for their income and expenses.

Perhaps the most important change for Bomani's future, however, is that new patterns of leadership and responsibility were established among the women. They learned that they can carry out an activity that is important to their community. They learned to work together, to assume and delegate responsibility, and to deal with authorities and agencies that provide access to the resources they need for further activities. More importantly, they learned to believe in their own abilities.

The original idea of building an oven developed to include a second oven, a bakery building, and a tea and bread kiosk. The women marketed their bread in other villages. Some women continued to make handicrafts for extra income and some learned new crafts. They considered starting a poultry project to provide eggs for the bakery and an additional source of income and food.

It was not easy, of course. Differing viewpoints had to be reconciled, and raising the money needed was very difficult. The group met weekly and there were continuous problems with those who arrived late or failed to attend. The women were strict, however, about their agreements, and with those who failed to keep them. Primarily, it was the women's growing enthusiasm that kept the project going. Both the co-ordinator and the facilitator fell ill; each was absent from one meeting and unable to lead the group in others because of 'fever and coughing'. The latrine shed the women were building fell down and they had to start all over again. There were problems with the bread at first, and the women who had originally learned to make it had to go back to Kanamai to learn how to measure ingredients. The women kept persevering and the project began to prosper. They decided to keep their money in the bank, rather than at the treasurer's home, in order to earn interest.

The women are proud of their achievement. They have gained a lot more than a way to earn some money. (IDRC, 1980)

Roman Catholic Mission Bakery in Botswana

A bakery was established by a Roman Catholic Mission which ran training courses for women who were unable to go to secondary school because of lack of good academic grades at primary school and/or because of lack of money. The sister in charge of the cooking/baking classes used to sell some of the surplus produce to people in the village. Out of this evolved the idea of building a bakery and employing some of the ex-trainees from the school.

Funds were obtained from the US Embassy Small Projects Fund by the Mission. Once the premises were completed, a manager was recruited to run the bakery and train at least two of the women in basic business administration skills and practical management of the bakery.

In a period of six to eight months, sales increased about five-fold. Small business owners came to the bakery and placed regular orders for loaves and scones, and even collected them daily by vehicle, while bread was delivered on foot to some nearby stores. For a while it was hard to cope with demand because of the small unplanned premises and the limited capacity of the oven (it would only turn out 40 loaves at a time).

The bakery employed ten women. The idea was to turn the bakery into a co-operative after it had been established for a while. The trainer discussed this idea with the women eight months after arriving. However, it seemed difficult for the women to understand what a co-operative was, and it was clear that they preferred to be employed rather than to employ. They saw the Mission as their employers. Promoting the idea of women as decision makers was not easy. On the other hand, they organized themselves very well in performing and co-ordinating the various daily tasks in the bakery. About 14 months after the bakery was established, bread sales dropped by 60 per cent in less than a week, and over the next few months continued to drop. A large bakery which had been operating in the capital, Gabarone, 370km to the south, had decided to expand production and sell bread to the whole eastern side of Botswana. The main reasons why the Mission's customers decided to switch to another supplier were as follows.

o The bread was slightly cheaper – the large bakery bought their flour direct from the mill in Pretoria, while the flour bought by the mission bakery passed through two wholesalers, each one taking a small cut.

o The bread was tightly wrapped in plastic by machine, which looked more attractive than the Mission bakery's plastic bread bags.

o The Gabarone plant delivered the bread direct to each shop, while theirs was delivered by hand, in baskets, or was collected by the customer.

o The shelf-life of the bread produced by the larger plant was about five days (because of preservative chemicals) while the Mission bakeries' bread only remained fresh for two to three days.

Royal Tropical Institute weaning food projects in Benin and Sierra Leone

It is generally recognized that in Africa, as in other parts of the South, many infants in the weaning period – the age between 6 and 30 months in which the infant changes from breastfeeding to the family pot – suffer from protein-energy malnutrition. Therefore young children need a special weaning food, providing nutrients to supplement their diet.

In many countries recipes based on local ingredients have been developed for home preparation but these have yielded very limited success. A number of factors inhibit mothers preparing weaning food at home: a lack of understanding of the necessity of a weaning food, ignorance of preparation techniques, seasonal availability of ingredients, as well as lack of time, fuel, and money. On top of these practical difficulties, home-prepared weaning foods have lower prestige and there may be other restricting cultural food habits. A low-cost ready-made weaning food of high nutritional quality can overcome these problems. Such a product, if it is acceptable to and affordable by broad sections of the population, can make an important contribution to improving the health of young children.

In the 1970s a number of projects were established in Africa to manufacture weaning foods locally. All were characterized by complex production processes relying on sophisticated technology and high investment, at best a simplified Western industrial process, at worst a complex project unsuited to local conditions and depending on expert mangement and maintenance. Such projects sometimes required imported raw materials which used up foreign exchange. The level of management competence required for their proper operation was unrealistically high for prevailing conditions.

With these adverse factors it is perhaps not surprising that almost all of these projects failed. Even during the enthusiastic start-up phase it became apparent that such projects could not become self-sufficient. Either the production plant or the final product required some degree of subsidy because the weaning foods were generally too expensive to reach any but a small elite of consumers.

At the Royal Tropical Institute, it became apparent that to have any chance of success where others had failed, it was important to develop a different approach that met several principal criteria.

○ A project should adapt to local conditions in the sense of using familiar patterns of work – domestic, craft-like, and collaborative.
○ It should be small in scale, easily understood, and not make too high demands on local management.
○ The final product ought to be acceptable to local tastes and, most importantly, be widely available at a price most people could afford.

Following these criteria, small-scale semi-industrial production units were established in Benin and Sierra Leone. They did not require sophisticated management or maintenance and they were designed to be self-supporting rather than requiring subsidy. In addition, they were based on the traditional African way of food preparation: made in batches and shared in a group. The process was simple although steps in the production process could be mechanized where feasible and, when a greater capacity was required, the existing set-up could be expanded. This approach has been shown to work in practice.

The weaning food manufactured in these plants is made of three basic ingredients with the mixture containing approximately 60 per cent cereals (rice, maize and sorghum), 15 per cent pulses (pigeon peas or cow peas) and 25 per cent oilseeds (peanut/groundnuts or sesame). If available, soya beans can be substituted for both oilseeds and pulses. If required, sugar may be added to sweeten the taste.

The process is basically composed of five steps: storage, cleaning/drying, roasting, mixing/milling, and packaging.

Storage

In tropical climates, special attention must be paid to pest-proof storage under hygienic conditions to avoid spoilage. This is crucial when the equivalent of an entire year's production requirements are bought at low post-harvest price to avoid later shortages and price rises. Cheap, effective, and simple methods are available such as the use of oil drums, which are generally available and can be hermetically sealed to become damp, insect, and rat-proof.

Cleaning and drying

The quality of the final product is largely determined by the thoroughness of cleaning. If machinery is used, hand-cleaning should always be used to finish the job. Groundnuts can be easily and safely cleaned by immersing in boiling salted water. This turns beans affected by aflatoxins a different colour so they can be removed. The undesirable constituents of soya beans can be easily dealt with by soaking and then steaming. All ingredients that have been washed should be thoroughly dried to avoid spoilage.

Roasting

The roasting process destroys enzymes, insects and bacteria. Thorough roasting improves the shelf-life of the finished product and promotes digestibility.

Mixing and milling

Batches of beans and cereals, mixed in the right proportions, can be milled into fine flour in a hammer mill. Because of their oily nature, the oilseeds should be milled separately then mixed with the cereal flour in a plate mill.

Packaging

Good packaging is essential to the final product which is sensitive to spoilage in tropical climates. A suitable material which is widely available is polyethylene. This gives a shelf-life of about a month.

Aluminium foil is better still, but is much more expensive and has to be imported.

Buildings should be simple in construction and easy to keep clean. Particular attention should be paid to details like the logical progress of work, easy access to stores, and protection against dust, heat and noise. Building layout should also be designed to allow for future expansion: a capacity of 100 tonnes per year is considered optimal; above this management might become too complicated. (Dijkhuizen *et al.*, undated)

Baby food in Tanzania

Researchers at the Tanzania Food and Nutrition Centre have found a way of preparing weaning food using the enzymes of germinating grains. In warm climates, grain that is moistened, and left for a few hours before grinding, starts to germinate (a process known as malting). Flour ground from malted grain is very rich in enzymes which break down starch to short-chain sugars. A spoonful of such flour added to a pot of stiff porridge can in a matter of minutes reduce it to a runny gruel, very rich in semi-digested carbohydrates, which is an ideal baby food. (*New Scientist*, 1986)

5
Checklist for project planning

ALTHOUGH THE CASE studies cover a limited number of experiences, they do provide an idea of the issues which need to be taken into consideration when designing a project involving the processing of cereals as a commercial venture. These include:

o the social organization and/or culture of the producers;
o the level of confidence of the producers in the feasibility of meeting the objectives and their willingness to risk and invest time and/or money and to take the risk;
o the process of identification of needs, and the level of conception of objectives on the part of the producers at the start of the project;
o extent of local adaptation/development and demonstration of the technology;
o existence of a market for the product;
o the existing production system and division of labour and the possible effects on them of the change introduced;
o technical, financial, administrative, book-keeping, marketing, management and organizational capacity of the producers;

o access of producers to credit, technical advice, and other training and information services;
o availability and accessibility of production and marketing infrastructure;
o year-round availability of and access to raw materials, fuel and water;
o capacity to produce a standard product from often non-uniform raw material;
o capacity to make integrated use of the available raw material and produce a range of products;
o local availability of necessary tools and equipment and mechanisms for national institutes/government to make necessary tools and equipment accessible;
o government policy in relation to marketing, export, import;
o macro-economic factors (for example, exchange rates, inflation).

The first questions are concerned with the viability of the enterprise; then there are questions about the role of women in traditional processing, with subsidiary questions listed below the main question where appropriate; and finally the impact of improved technologies is considered.

First questions

1. Why set up a small-scale cereal processing venture?
   o Is there a market for the products?
   o Can the existing system cope with increased demand?
   o If yes to the above, how will you improve/add capacity?
2. When processing a given quantity of cereals using the traditional process, what inputs are required?
   o How much time is required?
   o What is the labour input required from males and females for each activity or stage?

○ How much fuel is used, and is it readily available?
○ How much of the product is yielded?
○ What is the value of the inputs (raw materials, fuel, water, packaging) in comparison with the output?

Background questions

1. What exactly is the place of women in traditional processing? What role do they play in the different stages?
   ○ What is the traditional marketing mechanism and who controls it? (Do women have access to markets?)
   ○ What proportion of the income from the products do women earn and keep?
   ○ What are the major problems and difficulties of women producers in this field?
2. What is the extent of traditional and small-scale cereal processing in the area?
   ○ What are the traditional processes?
   ○ Are there different traditional processing methods?   Yes ☐   No ☐
   ○ Which method tends to be used most frequently, and why?
   ○ Does the main method vary in different parts of the country?
(It is important to know about the various traditional methods being used, as this may influence the improvements needed.)
3. Who owns the produce?
   ○ Is there more available than can be processed in the traditional manner?   Y ☐   N ☐
   ○ Are there ever seasonal shortages of cereals?   Y ☐   N ☐
   ○ What is done with the by-products?

Effects of improved technology

Technical considerations
1. Will the use of the improved technology reduce labour input as compared with the traditional method? How?
2. What is the capacity of the improved technology – will it be able to cope with the demands of processing in terms of quantity of cereals available to processors?
3. Will the equipment produce a greater quantity and better quality of the product than traditional means? (Will it have a different taste – if so, will it be acceptable?)
4. What will be the production rate?
5. Will the process be faster?   Y ☐   N ☐
6. What are the water/fuel/power requirements of the equipment?
7. Will the users be able to meet those requirements?   Y ☐   N ☐
8. Will use of the equipment require a change in packaging?   Y ☐   N ☐
   or transport of the product?   Y ☐   N ☐

9. If power-driven equipment is being introduced, can the users meet the electrical/diesel requirements on a regular basis? Y ☐   N ☐
10. Are there alternative energy sources? Y ☐   N ☐
11. Are there ways of producing equipment and/or spares locally? Y ☐   N ☐
12. Can the equipment be maintained using local resources?
    ○ are spare parts available? Y ☐   N ☐
    ○ can local artisans repair the machinery? Y ☐   N ☐ or do they need to be trained? Y ☐   N ☐
13. Will the users be able to afford the cost of spare parts? Y ☐   N ☐
14. Will the users of the equipment need to be trained?
    ○ will they need technical training Y ☐   N ☐ and if so, how much?
    ○ is training locally available? Y ☐   N ☐
    ○ is there already some familiarity with this type of technology? Y ☐   N ☐

Socio-economic considerations
1. What is the cost of the machine and related equipment?
2. Is the cost manageable on an individual or community basis?
3. If credit is needed is it accessible? Will the women be able to repay the loan?
4. What will the return on the investment be? What will the monthly profit be?
5. How many years will it take the operator to cover the cost of the machine?
6. Who will control use of the machine? Will it be co-operatively controlled or will individual men or women manage it?
7. Who will earn the income after processing?
8. Would availability of the improved technology increase women's income generation?
    ○ if not, why not?
    ○ what proportion of the income would women earn?
    ○ would cereal processing remain a significant income generating activity for women after introduction of the machine?
9. Will introduction of the equipment bring about any change in the pattern of work and work habits? How?
    ○ male
    ○ female
10. Will there be a change in the daily schedule required to do any task?
11. Does the improved equipment require more or less raw material than traditional methods?
12. If it requires more, is that supply available and who owns it?
13. Will the improved method change the traditional market mechanisms?
14. If more produce is processed, can the market cope with the increase and will this affect the price?
15. Will there be by-products from the improved method? What will happen to them?
16. If by-products are sold, who will earn the income?
17. Will the users be able to cope with the consequential requirements of effective enterprise development such as handling employees, market and price negotiations, and cash flow?

6
Tools and equipment

THIS SECTION AIMS to give a guide to the range of improved devices available for use in cereal processing projects/enterprises in the categories described in Chapter 2.

Types of equipment available for cereal processing

Winnowers
o Cecoco

Shellers/Decorticators
o Atlas
o Chitetze

Threshers
o Treadle
o Cecoco

Stone mills and plate mills
o Dandekar stone mill
o Ndume grinding mill
o Atlas No. 1 plate mill

Hammer mills
o Ndume
o MGM

Hullers
o PRL/RIIC
o Engleberg
o Cecoco rubber-roller

Driers
o IRRI batch drier

A range of available equipment is described to suit various needs and circumstances. Details are given on the size, capacity, and manufacturing requirements of each piece of equipment. This is aimed at helping consultants and project managers to decide whether something exists which is appropriate to local needs and circumstances, and to converse on more equal terms with the technologists who are needed to supply the technical solutions.

Although only a limited number of machines are described here, they are chosen to indicate the range available. The information is based on references found in books and private communications with individuals in different organizations. As far as possible, equipment that is made in developing countries is included, but this is also limited. Any additional information or comments would be welcome.

Before ordering any equipment it would be beneficial to consult appropriate institutions (listed in the Contacts section), especially those who have had previous experience in introducing the equipment.

Winnowers

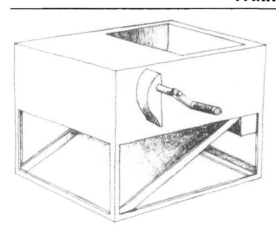

Cecoco
Processes: cereals
Power source: manual
Capacity: 650kg/h
Suitable: small-scale farmer
Manufacture requirements: Sheet metal and angle iron
Comments: many manual winnowers can be adapted to be motor-driven. (Fellows and Hampton, 1992)

Shellers

Atlas sheller

Processes: maize
Power source: manual
Capacity: 56kg cobs giving 48.5kg/h kernels, 5.8 rotations per cob.
Suitable: small-scale farmer
Manufacture requirements: castings
Comments: easy to operate; sometimes extra pushing of the cob is needed; few breakages. (Mphuru, 1982)

Chitetze maize sheller

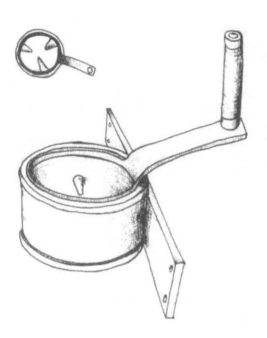

Processes: maize
Power source: manual
Capacity: 45kg/h
Suitable: small-scale farmer
Manufacture requirements: metal workshop, welding
Comments: the shellers are made in three sizes to suit the principal maize varieties in Malawi. (Carruthers and Rodriguez, 1992)

Threshers

Treadle

Processes: most types of grain
Power source: manual
Capacity: 25–30kg/h
Suitable: small-scale and large-scale farmer
Comments: although the thresher can be used for most grains it is particularly suitable for paddy. (Carruthers and Rodriguez, 1992)

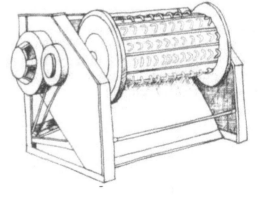

Cecoco

Processes: paddy
Power source: pedal/motor
Capacity: 90–130kg/h
Suitable: large-scale farmer
Comments: operated by a foot pedal.

Stone mills and plate mills

Dandekar stone mill

Processes: most cereals and pulses
Power source: 6–10hp motor
Capacity: 225–270kg/h
Suitable: custom milling, co-operative
Comments: Manufactured in India, this mill is particularly suitable for fine grinding.

Ndume grinding mill

Processes: maize
Power source: manual
Capacity: 20kg/h
Suitable: small-scale farmer
Manufacture requirements: metal work-shop, welding, plates need casting
Comments: made in Kenya, but can be manufactured locally; not suitable for fine grinding.

Atlas No. 1 plate mill

Processes: dry grain
Power source: manual
Capacity: 7–9kg/h
Suitable: small-scale farmer
Manufacture requirements: casting
Comments: smaller mill than that de-scribed in case study.

Hammer mills

Ndume

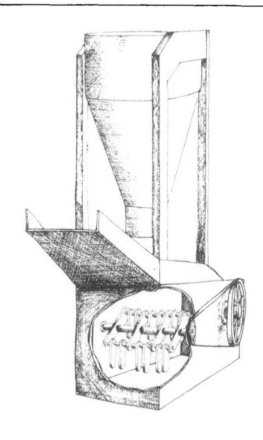

Processes: maize, sorghum, millet
Power source: electric motor/diesel engine
(2–20hp)
Capacity: 70–200kg/h for small unit, 400–
2500kg/h large unit
Suitable: large-scale farmer, co-operative
Comments: if skill and manufacturing requirements are available then hammer
mills can be made locally, as this one has
been in Kenya. (ECA Publications, 1985)

MGM

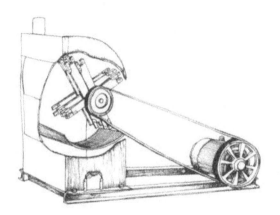

Processes: maize, sorghum, millet
Power source: diesel engines, 8–12hp
Capacity: 180–200kg/h
Suitable: large-scale farmer, co-operative
Comments: four different models of the
MGM series are available with various
capacities from Tanzania. (ECA Publica-
tions, 1985)

Hullers

PRL/RIIC

Processes: sorghum, millet
Power source: electric motor/diesel engine
Suitable: large-scale farmer, co-operative
Comments: modifications at RIIC (in Botswana) enable this machine to be used either on a continuous or batch operated basis (see Chapter 2 and case study). (Fellows and Hampton, 1992)

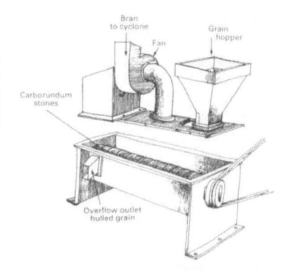

Engleberg

Processes: rice
Power source: electric motor/diesel engine 3–15hp
Capacity: 30–300kg/h paddy
Suitable: large-scale farmer, co-operative

Comments: more robust than rubber-roller mills, has fewer maintenance problems and lasts longer; breaks up the grain – but in some villages broken grains do not matter. (Carruthers and Rodriguez, 1992)

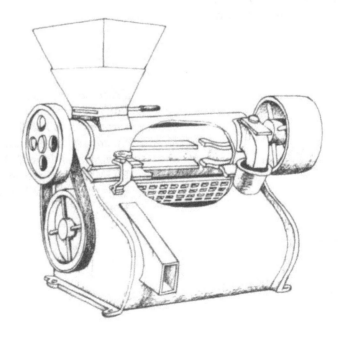

Cecoco rubber-roller

Processes: paddy
Power source: electric motor/diesel engine
5–7hp
Capacity: 360kg/h paddy
Suitable: large-scale farmer, co-operative
Comments: gives a good quality grain and
is efficient mechanically, but it is not re-
commended for small-scale operation because it is expensive and needs frequent
replacement of parts. A manual design is
also available from Cecoco. (Carruthers
and Rodriguez, 1992)

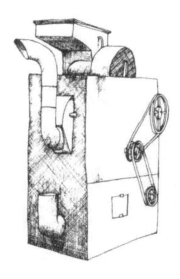

Driers

IRRI batch drier

Processes: paddy and other grains
Power source: petrol/kerosene engine,
electric motor or rice husk burner
Capacity: 1 tonne
Suitable: medium-scale farmer, co-
operative
Comments: good general purpose drier
that could be locally manufactured.

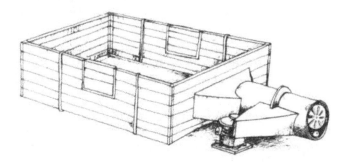

References

Cain, M. (1981) in Dauber, R. and Cain, M. (eds) *Women and Technological Change in Developing Countries*, Westview Press, Connecticut, USA.

Carruthers, I. and Rodriguez, M. (1992) *Tools for Agriculture: A guide to appropriate equipment for smallholder farmers.* IT Publications, London.

Dichter, D. (1978) *Manual on Imported Farm and Village-level Grain Storage Methods,* GATE/GTZ, Eschborn, Germany.

Dijkhuizen, P., Korthals Altes, F.W. and Merz, R. (undated) *A New Approach to Small-Scale Food Production from Indigenous Raw Material in Tropical Countries,* Royal Tropical Institute, Amsterdam, Netherlands.

ECA Publications (1983) *Traditional Palm Oil Processing: Women's role and the application appropriate technology,* ATRCW Research Series, Addis Ababa, Ethiopia.

ECA Publications (1985) *Technical Compendium on Composite Flours,* Addis Ababa, Ethiopia.

FAO, Rome (1970) *Handling and Storage of Food Grains.*

FAO, Rome (undated) *The Lost Harvest.*

Fellows, P. and Hampton, A. (1992) *Small-scale Food Processing: A guide to appropriate equipment.* IT Publications, London, UK.

Fennelly Levy, M. *Bringing women into the Community Development Process: A pragmatic approach,* Occasional Paper no. 2, Save the Children.

Golob, P., (1977) *TPI Rural Technology Guide No. 3,* TPI Publications, London, UK.

Hemmings-Gapihan, G.S. (1981) in Dauber, R. and Cain, M. (eds), *Women and Technological Change in Developing Countries.* 'Baseline Study for Socio-Economic Evaluation of Tangaye Solar Site'.

Ihekoronye, A. and Ngoddy, P.O. (1985) *Integrated Food Science and Technology for the Tropics,* Macmillan, London, UK.

ILO/JASPA (1981) *Appropriate Technologies in Cereal Milling and Fruit Processing Industries,* Addis Ababa, Ethiopia.

Khan, S.D. (1982) *Evaluation Report on Trainers' Training Programme for Women Group Leaders of Grameen Bank Project,* Oct. 1982, Grameen Bank, Dhaka, Bangladesh.

Loose, E. (1979) *Women in Rural Senegal: Some economic and social observations,* Paper prepared for the Workshop on Sahelian Agriculture, Purdue University, 1979.

McSweeney, B. (1982) *'Time to Learn for Women in Upper Volta'. Appropriate Technology Journal*, Vol. 9, No. 3, IT Publications, London, UK.

Mphuru, A.N. (1982) *On-Farm Handling, Processing and Storage of Food Grains in Africa.* Africa Regional Centre for Technology (ARCT), Dakar, Senegal.

NAS (1978) *Post-Harvest Food Losses in Developing Countries.* National Academy of Sciences, Washington DC, USA.

New Scientist (1986) *New Scientist,* 2 January 1986, London, UK.

O'Kelly, E. (1973) *Aid and Self-Help.* Knight and Co., London, UK.

Peace Corps/VITA (1977) *Small Farm Grain Storage*, Vol. III.

IDRC (1980) *A Bakery for Bomani*, IDRC Reports, July 1980.

SCF/CDF (1980) *A Case Presentation of Save the Children Federation Community Development Foundation*, Save the Children, Occasional Paper No. 2, USA.

Scott, G. and Carr, M. (1985) *The Impact of Technology Choice on Rural Women in Bangladesh: Problems and opportunities*, World Bank, Washington DC, USA.

Siegel, A. (1976) *Maiduguri Mill Project*, IDRC Mimeo.

Spurgeon, D. *A Systems Approach to Post-Harvest Technology*, PAG Bulletin, Vol. VII, No. 1–2.

Stewart, F. (1978) *Technology and Underdevelopment*, Macmillan, London, UK.

UNICEF (1983) *UNICEF News*.

Whitby, G. (1985) 'Successfully Processing Sorghum'. *Appropriate Technology Journal*, Vol. 12, No. 1, IT Publications, London, UK.

Further reading

Wageningen Agricultural University (1983) *Selection of Technology for Food Processing in Developing Countries*, Pudoc, Wageningen, The Netherlands.

The International Rice Research Institute, Manila, Philippines (1985) *Women in Rice Farming*, Gower Publications, London, UK.

World Employment Programme (1984) *Technological Change, Basic Needs and the Condition of Rural Women*, ILO, Geneva, Switzerland.

FAO (1983) *Processing and Storage of Food by Rural Families*, Rome, Italy.

FAO (1985) *Manual on the Establishment, Operation and Management of Cereal Banks*, Rome, Italy.

ILO (1984) *Small-Scale Maize Milling*, Technology Memorandum No. 7, Geneva, Switzerland.

ILO (1984) *Improved Village Technology for Women's Activities*, Geneva, Switzerland.

IDRC (1980) *An End to Pounding: A mechanical flour milling system in use in Africa*, Ottawa, Canada.

Kent, N.L. (1975) *Technology of Cereals with Special Reference to Wheat*, 2nd edn, Pergamon Press, London, UK.

IDRC (1982) *Sorghum Milling in Botswana: A development impact case study*, Ottawa, Canada.

FAO (1983) *Expert Consultation on Women in Food Production*, Rome, Italy.

Merrick Lockwood, L. (1981) *Development and Testing of a Portable Rice Huller for Bangladesh*, The Asia Foundation, Dhaka, Bangladesh.

Association of Development Agencies in Bangladesh (1980) *ADAB News*, Post-Harvest Technology, Vol. VII, No. 11, Nov. 1980.

Gariboldi, F. (1974) *Rice Parboiling*, Rome, Italy.

Greeley, M. and Howes, M. (1982) *Rural Technology, Rural Institutions, and the Rural Poorest: The case of rice processing in Bangladesh*, CIRDAP/Institute of Development Studies (IDS), University of Sussex, UK.

Harriss, B. (1978) 'Rice Processing Projects in Bangladesh: An Appraisal of a decade of proposals'. *The Bangladesh Journal of Agricultural Economics*, Vol. 1, No. 2, December 1978.

Harriss, B. (1979) 'Post-Harvest Rice Processing Systems in Rural Bangladesh: Technology, economics and employment', *The Bangladesh Journal of Agricultural Economics*, Vol. 2, No. 1, June 1979.

'Paddy Processing in India and Sri Lanka: a Review of the case for technological innovation'. *Tropical Science*, 1976.

Contacts

The following can be contacted for further information about cereal processing and planning cereal processing projects. Some of these institutions have developed their own equipment which has been or is being used in the field.

ADA
Agricultural Development Authority, Enugu, Anambra State, Nigeria.

ATI
Appropriate Technology International, 1724 Massachusetts Ave. NW, Washington DC 20036, USA.

CAMERTEC
Centre for Agricultural Mechanization and Rural Technology, PO Box 764, Arusha, Tanzania.

CDTF
Community Development Trust Fund, PO Box 9421, Dar es Salaam, Tanzania.

CIMMYT
Centro Internacional de Mejoramiento de Maiz y Trigo, Bueno Lisboa 27, Apdo Postal 6-641, 06600 Mexico City, Mexico.

FAO
Food and Agriculture Organization, Via delle Terme di Caracalla, 00100 Rome, Italy.

GATE/GTZ
German Appropriate Technology Exchange, Postfach 5180, D-6236 Eschborn 1, Germany.

GRET
Groupe de Recherche et d'Echanges Technologiques, 213 rue Lafayette, Paris 75010, France.

ICRISAT
International Crops Research Institute for Semi-Arid Tropics, Pantachero PO, Hyderabad, Andhra Pradesh 502 324, India; and BP 12404, Niamey, Niger.

IDRC
International Development Research Centre, Box 8500, Ottawa, K1G 3H9, Canada.

IDS
Institute of Development Studies, University of Sussex, Brighton BN1 9RE, UK.

IITA
International Institute of Tropical Agriculture, PMB 5320, Ibadan, Nigeria.
ILO
International Labour Office, CH 1211 Geneva 22, Switzerland.
IRRI
International Rice Research Institute, PO Box 933, Manila, Philippines.
Intermediate Technology
Myson House, Railway Terrace, Rugby, CV21 3HT UK
KIT
Royal Tropical Institute, Mauritskade 63, 1092 AD, Amsterdam, The Netherlands.
NRI
Natural Resources Institute (formerly known as TDRI), Central Avenue, Chatham Maritime, Chatham ME4 4TB, UK.
RIIC
Rural Industries Innovation Centre, Private Bag 11, Kanye, Botswana.
University of Nigeria
Department of Food Science and Technology, Nsukka, Anambra, Nigeria.
UST
University of Science and Technology, Faculty of Agriculture, Department of Engineering, Kumasi, Ghana.
VITA
Volunteers in Technical Assistance, 1600 Wilson Boulevard, Suite 500, PO Box 1238, Arlington, Virginia 22209, USA.
WARDA
West African Rice Development Association, PO Box 1019, Monrovia, Liberia.